AWS: Security Best Practices on AWS

Delve deep into various ~~~~ty aspects of AWS
to build and maintain a ~~~~ environment

Albert Anthony

BIRMINGHAM - MUMBAI

AWS: Security Best Practices on AWS

First published: March 2018

Production reference: 1070318

Published by Packt Publishing Ltd.
Livery Place, 35 Livery Street
Birmingham B3 2PB, UK.

ISBN: 978-1-78913-451-3

www.packtpub.com

Credits

This book is a blend of text and quizzes, all packaged up keeping your journey in mind. It includes content from the following Packt product:

- *Mastering AWS Security* by *Albert Anthony*

Meet Your Expert

We have the best work of the following esteemed author to ensure that your learning journey is smooth:

Albert Anthony is a seasoned IT professional with 18 years of experience working with various technologies and in multiple teams spread all across the globe. He believes that the primary purpose of information technology is to solve problems faced by businesses and organizations. He is an AWS certified solutions architect and a corporate trainer. He holds all three AWS associate-level certifications along with PMI-PMP and Certified Scrum Master certifications. He has been training since 2008 on project management, cost management, and people management, and on AWS since 2016. He has managed multiple projects on AWS that runs big data applications, hybrid mobile application development, DevOps, and infrastructure monitoring on AWS. He has successfully migrated multiple workloads to AWS from on premise data centers and other hosting providers. He is responsible for securing workloads for all his customers, with hundreds of servers; processing TBs of data; and running multiple web, mobile, and batch applications.

Table of Contents

Preface

With organizations moving their workloads, applications, and infrastructure to the cloud at an unprecedented pace, security of all these resources has been a paradigm shift for all those who are responsible for security; experts, novices, and apprentices alike. AWS provides many controls to secure customer workloads and quite often customers are not aware of their share of security responsibilities, and the security controls that they need to own and put in place for their resources in the AWS cloud.

What's in It for Me?

Maps are vital for your journey, especially when you're holidaying in another continent. When it comes to learning, a roadmap helps you in giving a definitive path for progressing towards the goal. So, here you're presented with a roadmap before you begin your journey.

This book is meticulously designed and developed in order to empower you with all the right and relevant information on AWS. We've created this Learning Path for you that consists of five lessons:

Lesson 1, AWS Virtual Private Cloud, talks about creating and securing our own virtual network in the AWS cloud. This lesson also introduces you to the various connectivity options that AWS provides to create hybrid cloud, public cloud, and private cloud solutions.

Lesson 2, Data Security in AWS, covers encryption in AWS to secure your data in rest and while working with AWS data storage services.

Lesson 3, Securing Servers in AWS, explains ways to secure your infrastructure in AWS by employing continuous threat assessment, agent-based security checks, virtual firewalls for your servers, and so on.

Lesson 4, Securing Applications in AWS, introduces you to ways to secure all your applications developed and deployed in the AWS environment. You will walk through the web application firewall service, as well as securing a couple of AWS services used by developers for web and mobile application development.

Lesson 5, AWS Security Best Practices, walks you through best practices in a consolidated form for securing all your resources in AWS.

What Will I Get from This Book?

- Get familiar with VPC components, features, and benefits
- Learn to create and secure your private network in AWS
- Explore encryption and decryption fundamentals
- Understand monitoring, logging, and auditing in AWS
- Ensure data security in AWS
- Secure your web and mobile applications in AWS
- Learn security best practices for IAM, VPC, shared security responsibility model, and so on

Prerequisites

This book is for all IT professionals, system administrators, security analysts, solution architects, and chief information security officers who are responsible for securing workloads in AWS for their organizations. Some of the prerequisites that is required before you begin this book are:

- Working knowledge on AWS is required
- Working knowledge of Linux is assumed

1

AWS Virtual Private Cloud

Amazon Virtual Private Cloud or VPC, as it is popularly known, is a logically separated, isolated, and secure virtual network on the cloud, where you provision your infrastructure, such as Amazon RDS instances and Amazon EC2 instances. It is a core component of networking services on AWS cloud.

A VPC is dedicated to your AWS account. You can have one or more VPCs in your AWS account to logically isolate your resources from each other. By default, any resource provisioned in a VPC is not accessible by the internet unless you allow it through AWS-provided firewalls. A VPC spans an AWS region.

VPC is essentially your secure private cloud within AWS public cloud. It is specifically designed for users who require an extra layer of security to protect their resources on the cloud. It segregates your resources with other resources within your AWS account. You can define your network topology as per your requirements, such as if you want some of your resources hidden from public or if you want resources to be accessible from the internet.

Getting the design of your VPC right is absolutely critical for having a secure, fault-tolerant, and scalable architecture.

It resembles a traditional network in a physical data center in many ways, for example, having similar components such as subnets, routes, and firewalls; however, it is a software-defined network that performs the job of data centers, switches, and routers. It is primarily used to transport huge volume of packets into, out of, and across AWS regions in an optimized and secured way along with segregating your resources as per their access and connectivity requirements. And because of these features, VPC does not need most of the traditional networking and data center gear.

VPC gives you granular control to define what traffic flows in or out of your VPC.

Introduction

In this lesson, we will deep dive into the security of AWS VPC. VPC is the most important component of networking services in AWS. Networking services are one of the foundation services on the AWS cloud. A secure network is imperative to ensure security in AWS for your resources.

We will look at components that make up VPC, such as subnets, security groups, various gateways, and so on. We will take a deep dive into the AWS VPC features and benefits such as simplicity, security, multiple connectivity options, and so on.

We will look at the following most popular use cases of VPC that use various security and connectivity features of VPC:

- Hosting a public-facing website
- Hosting multi-tier web applications
- Creating branch office and business unit networks
- Hosting web applications in AWS cloud that are connected with your data center
- Extending corporate network on the cloud
- Disaster recovery

AWS provides multiple measures to secure resources in VPC and monitor activities in VPC, such as security groups, network **access control list (ACL)**, and VPC flow logs. We will dive deep into each of these measures.

Next, we'll walk through the process of creating a VPC. You can either choose to create a VPC through the wizard, through the console, or through the CLI.

Furthermore, we'll go through the following VPC connectivity options along with VPC limits in detail:

- Network to AWS VPC
- AWS VPC to AWS VPC
- Internal user to AWS VPC

We'll wrap up this lesson with VPC best practices.

Throughout this lesson, we'll take a look at AWS architecture diagrams for various use cases, connectivity options, and features. The objective of this lesson is to familiarize you with AWS VPC and let you know about ways to secure your VPC.

VPC Components

AWS VPC is a logically separated network isolated from other networks. It lets you set your own IP address range and configure security settings and routing for all your traffic. AWS VPC is made up of several networking components, as shown in the following figure; some of them are as follows:

- Subnets
- Elastic network interfaces
- Route tables
- Internet gateways
- Elastic IP addresses
- VPC endpoints
- NAT
- VPC peering

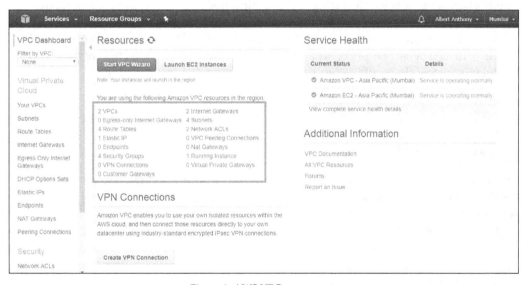

Figure 1: AWS VPC components

Let's take a closer look at these components:

Subnets

A VPC spans an AWS region. A region contains two or more availability zones. A VPC contains subnets that are used to logically separate resources inside a region. A subnet cannot span across multiple availability zones. A subnet can either be a private subnet or a public subnet based on its accessibility from outside of VPC and if it can access resources outside of VPC.

Subnets are used for separating resources, such as web servers and database servers. They are also used for making your application highly available and fault-tolerant. By default, all resources in all subnets of a VPC can route (communicate) to each other using private IP addresses.

Elastic Network Interfaces (ENI)

The ENI are available for EC2 instances running inside a VPC. An ENI can have many attributes, such as a primary private IPv4 address, a MAC address, one or more security groups, one or more IPv6 addresses, and so on. These attributes will move with ENI when an ENI is attached to an instance; when this ENI is detached from an instance, these attributes will be removed.

By default, every VPC has a network interface attached to every instance. This ENI is known as a primary network interface (eth0). This default ENI cannot be detached from an instance. You can, however, create and attach many additional ENIs to your instances inside a VPC.

One of the popular use cases of ENI is having secondary ENI attached to instances running network and security appliances, such as network address translation servers or load balancers. These ENIs can be configured with their own attributes, such as public and private IP address, security groups, and so on.

Route Tables

As you've learned about VPC, it essentially facilitates traffic in and out of a software-defined network. This traffic needs to know where to go, and this is achieved via route tables. A route table in VPC has rules or routes defined for the flow of traffic. Every VPC has a default route table that is known as the main route table. You can modify this main route table and you can create additional route tables.

Each subnet in VPC is associated with only one route table, however, one route table can be attached to multiple subnets. You use route tables to decide what data stays inside of VPC and what data should go outside of VPC, and that is where it plays a very important part in deciding data flow for a VPC.

In the following figure, you can see four route tables for two VPCs in my AWS account. You can see rules in the route table, and you see tabs for subnet associations as well:

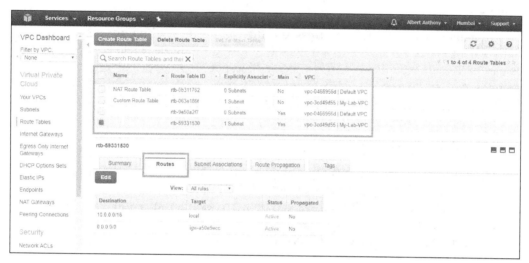

Figure 2: AWS VPC route tables

Internet Gateway

An internet gateway allows communication between resources such as EC2 and RDS instances in your VPC and the Internet. It is highly available, redundant, and horizontally scalable; that is, you do not need to attach more than one internet gateway to your VPC in order to support an increase in traffic.

An internet gateway serves as a target for route table in VPC for all the traffic that is supposed to go out of VPC to the internet. Along with that, it also performs network address translation for all instances with public IPv4 addresses.

Elastic IP Addresses

An Elastic IP Address is a public IPv4, static address that can be associated with any one instance or one network interface at a time within any VPC in your AWS account. When your application is dependent on an IP address, you would use an Elastic IP address instead of a regular public IP address because public IP addresses would be lost if the underlying instance shuts down for some reason. You can simply move your Elastic IP address to another instance that is up and running from a failed instance.

You first allocate an Elastic IP address and then associate it with your instance or network interface. Once you do not need it, you should disassociate it and then release it. If an Elastic IP address is allocated but not associated with any instance, then you will be charged by AWS on an hourly basis, so if you don't have a requirement for Elastic IP addresses, it is better to release them.

VPC Endpoints

A VPC endpoints is a secure way to communicate with other AWS services without using the internet, Direct Connect, VPN Connection, or a NAT device. This communication happens within the Amazon network internally so your traffic never goes out of Amazon network. At present, endpoints are supported only for **Simple Storage Service (S3)**. These endpoints are virtual devices supporting IPv4-only traffic.

An endpoint uses the private IP address of instances in your VPC to communicate with other services. You can have more than one endpoint in your VPC. You create a route in your route table for directing traffic from instance V2 in subnet 2 through your endpoint to your target service (such as S3), as shown in the following figure:

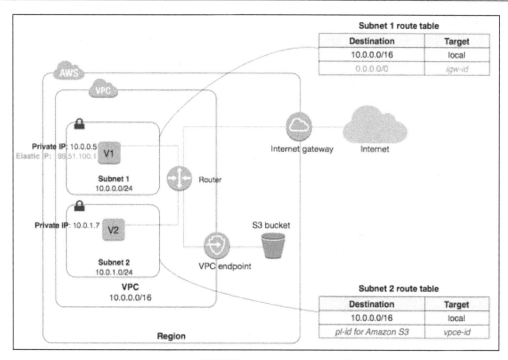

Figure 3: AWS VPC endpoints and route tables

Network Address Translation (NAT)

You will often have resources in your VPC that will reside in private subnets that are not accessible from the internet. However, these resources will need to access the internet occasionally for patch update, software upgrade, and so on. A NAT device is used exactly for this purpose, allowing resources in private subnet to connect with either the internet or other AWS services securely. NAT devices support only IPv4 traffic.

AWS offers a NAT gateway, a managed device, and a NAT instance as NAT devices. Depending on your use case, you will choose either of them. AWS recommends a NAT gateway over a NAT instance as it is a managed service that requires little or no administration, is highly available, and highly scalable.

VPC Peering

You can connect your VPC with one or more VPCs in the same region through the VPCs peering option. This connection enables you to communicate with other VPC using private IPv4 or private IPv6 addresses. Since this is a networking connection, instances in these VPCs can communicate with each other as if they are in the same network.

You can peer with VPCs in your AWS account or VPCs in other AWS accounts as well. Transitive peering is not allowed and VPCs should not have overlapping or matching IPv4 or IPv6 CIDR blocks. The following figure shows VPC peering between VPC A and VPC B. Note that the CIDR blocks differ for these two VPCs:

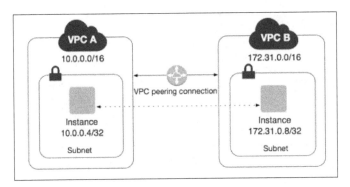

Figure 4: AWS VPC peering

VPC Features and Benefits

AWS VPC offers many features and benefits to secure your resources in your own virtual network on the cloud. You can scale your resources and select resources as per your requirement in VPC just like you do in AWS, with the same level of reliability and additional security. Let's look at these features and benefits.

Multiple Connectivity Options

Your AWS VPC can be connected to a variety of resources, such as the internet, your on-premise data center, other VPCs in your AWS account, or VPCs in other AWS accounts; once connected, you can make your resources accessible or inaccessible in your VPC from outside of your VPC based on your requirement.

You can allow your instances in your VPC to connect with the internet directly by launching them in a subnet that is publicly accessible, also known as a public subnet. This way, your instances can send and receive traffic from the internet directly.

For instances in private subnets that are not publicly accessible, you can use a NAT device placed in a public subnet to access the internet without exposing their private IP address.

You can connect your VPC to your corporate data center by creating a secure VPN tunnel using encrypted IPsec hardware VPN connection. Once connected, all traffic between instances in your VPC and your corporate data center will be secured via this industry standard hardware VPN connection.

You can connect your VPC with other VPCs privately in the same region through the VPC peering feature. This way, you can share resources in your VPC with other virtual networks across your AWS accounts or other AWS accounts.

The VPC endpoint is used to connect to AWS services such as S3 without using internet gateway or NAT. You can also configure what users or resources are allowed to connect to these AWS services.

You can mix and match the mentioned options to support your business or application requirements. For example, you can connect VPC to your corporate data center using a hardware VPN connection, and you can allow instances in your public subnet to connect directly with the internet as well. You can configure route tables in your VPC to direct all traffic to its appropriate destination.

Secure

AWS VPC has security groups that act as an instance-level firewall and network ACLS that act as a subnet-level firewall. These advanced security features allow you to configure rules for incoming and outgoing traffic for your instances and subnets in your VPC.

With help of the VPC endpoint, you can enable access control for your data in AWS S3 so that only instances in your VPC can access that data. You can also launch dedicated instances to have isolation at the instance level; these instances have dedicated hardware for a single customer.

Simple

AWS VPC can be created using AWS Management Console in a couple of ways; you can either create it through `Start VPC Wizard`, or you can create it manually as well. You can also create VPC from AWS command-line interface.

VPC wizard gives you multiple options to create VPC, as shown in the following figure; you can pick one that suits your requirements and customize it later if needed. When you create a VPC using VPC wizard, all components of VPC, such as security groups, route tables, subnets and so on, are automatically created by VPC wizard:

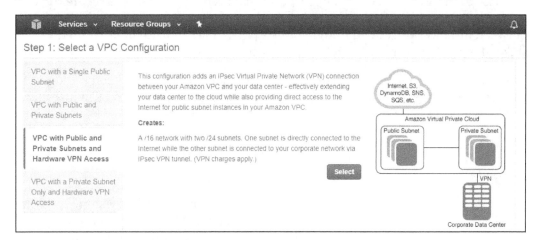

Figure 5: AWS VPC wizard

VPC Use Cases

With VPC, you can control inbound and outbound access for your resources in your own virtual private network and connect your data center with AWS cloud securely along with other VPCs in your AWS accounts and VPCs in other AWS accounts. You can also securely access data on S3 from your resources in VPC without using the internet.

All these along with many other features make VPC a preferred choice for a variety of use cases, such as hosting development and testing environments in AWS VPC. You could also use VPC for creating environments for **Proof of Concept (PoC)**. These environments can be created on short notice and could act as an isolated network accessible only by specific teams or other resources. Since VPC is a software-defined network, it brings loads of flexibility in designing, integrating, and securing your resources in AWS cloud.

Let's look at some of the most popular use cases for VPC.

Hosting a Public Facing Website

You can host a public facing website, which could be a blog, a single tier simple web application, or just a simple website using VPC. You can create a public subnet using the VPC wizard and select the VPC with a single public subnet only option, or you can create it manually. Secure your website using instance-level firewalls, known as security groups, allowing inbound traffic, either HTTP or HTTPS, from the internet and restricting outbound traffic to the internet when required at the same time.

Hosting Multi-Tier Web Application

Hosting a multi-tier web application requires stricter access control and more restrictions for communication between your servers for layers, such as web servers, app servers, and database servers. VPC is an ideal solution for such web applications as it has all functionalities built in.

In the following figure, there is one public subnet that contains the web server and the application server. These two instances need to have inbound and outbound access for internet traffic. This public subnet also has one NAT instance that is used to route traffic for database instance in the private subnet.

The private subnet holds instances that do not need to have access to the internet. They only need to communicate with instances in the public subnet. When an instance in the private subnet needs to access the internet for downloading patches or software update, it will do that via a NAT instance placed in the public subnet:

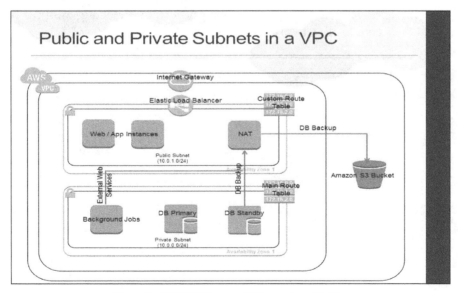

Figure 6: AWS VPC for a multi-tier web application

Access control for this sort of architecture is configured using network ACLs that act as a firewall for subnets. You will also use security groups for configuring access at the instance level, allowing inbound and outbound access.

The VPC wizard gives you an option, **VPC with Public and Private Subnets**, to support this use case; alternatively, you can create a VPC using AWS console manually or through a command-line interface.

Creating Branch Office and Business Unit Networks

Quite often, there is a requirement for connecting branch offices with their own, interconnected networks. This requirement can be fulfilled by provisioning instances within a VPC with a separate subnet for different branch offices. All resources within a VPC can communicate with each other through a private IP address by default, so all offices will be connected to each other and will also have their own local network within their own subnet.

If you need to limit communication across subnets for some instances, you can use security groups to configure access for such instances. These rules and designs can be applied to applications that are used by multiple offices within an organization. These common applications can be deployed within a VPC in a public subnet and can be configured so that they are accessible only from branch offices within an organization by configuring NACLs that acts as a firewall for subnets.

The following figure shows an example of using VPC for connecting multiple branch offices with their own local networks:

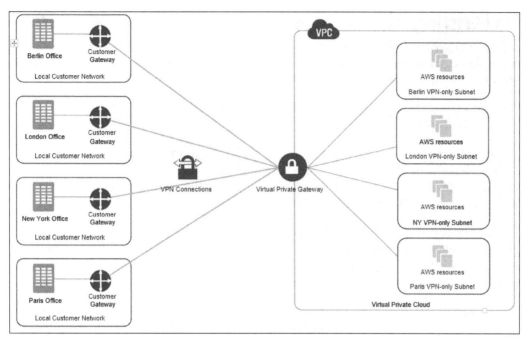

Figure 7: AWS VPC for connecting branch offices

Hosting Web Applications in the AWS Cloud That Are Connected with Your Data Center

Through VPC, you can also support scenarios where instances in one subnet allow inbound and outbound access to the internet and instances in other subnet can communicate exclusively with resources in your corporate data center. You will secure these communications by creating an IPsec hardware VPN connection between your VPC and your corporate network.

In this scenario, you can host your web applications in the AWS cloud in VPC and you can sync data with databases in your corporate data center through the VPN tunnel securely.

You can create a VPC for this use case using the VPC wizard and selecting **VPC with Public and Private Subnets and Hardware VPN Access**. You can also create a VPC manually through the AWS console or through the CLI.

Extending Corporate Network in AWS Cloud

This use case is specifically useful if you have a consistent requirement for provisioning additional resources, such as compute, storage, or database capacity to your existing infrastructure based on your workload.

This use case is also applicable to all those data centers that have reached their peak capacity and don't have room to extend further.

You can extend your corporate networking resources in the AWS cloud and take all benefits of cloud computing such as elasticity, pay-as-you-go model, security, high availability, minimal or no capex, and instant provisioning of resources by connecting your VPC with your corporate network.

You can host your VPC behind the firewall of your corporate network and ensure you move your resources to the cloud without impacting user experience or the performance of your applications. You can keep your corporate network as is and scale your resources up or down in the AWS cloud based on your requirements.

You can define your own IP address range while creating an AWS VPC, so extending your network into a VPC is similar to extending your existing corporate network in your physical data center.

To support this use case, you can create a VPC by opting for the **VPC with a Private Subnet Only and Hardware VPN Access** option in the VPC wizard or create a VPC manually. You can either connect your VPC to your data center using hardware VPN or through AWS direct connect service. The following figure shows an example of a data center extended in AWS cloud through VPC using an existing internet connection. It uses a hardware VPN connection for connecting the data center with AWS VPC.

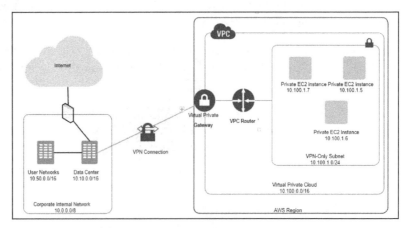

Figure 8: AWS VPC extend corporate data center

Disaster Recovery

As part of your **disaster recovery** (**DR**) and business continuity plan, you will need to continuously back up your critical data to your DR site. You can use a VPC to host EC2 instances with EBS volumes and store data in S3 buckets as well as in EBS volumes attached to EC2 instances securely, which can be configured to be accessible only from your network.

As part of your business continuity plan, you might want to run a small set of EC2 instances in your VPC, and these EC2 instances could be scaled quickly to meet the demand of a production workload in the event of a disaster. When the disaster is over, you could replicate data back to your data center and use servers in the data center to run your workload. Post that, you can terminate additionally provisioned resources, such as EC2 instances and RDS instances in AWS VPC.

You can plan your disaster recovery and business continuity with AWS VPC at a fraction of the cost of a traditional co-location site using physical data center. Moreover, you can automate your disaster recovery and business continuity plan using the AWS CloudFormation service; this automation will drastically reduce your deployment and provisioning time in AWS VPC when compared with a traditional physical data center.

VPC Security

AWS VPC essentially carries out the task of moving IP traffic (packets) into, out of, and across AWS regions; so, the first line of defense for a VPC is to secure what traffic can enter and leave your VPC. All resources can communicate with each other within a VPC unless explicitly configured not to do that, so this leaves us primarily with securing communication outside of your VPC with resources inside your VPC and vice versa.

AWS VPC provides multiple features for securing your VPC and securing resources inside your VPC, such as security groups, network ACL, VPC Flow Logs, and controlling access for VPC. These features act as additional layers of defense while designing your VPC architecture and are used to increase security and monitor your VPC. Apart from these features, you have a routing layer available in the form of route tables.

These features enable us to implement a layered defense for an in-depth security architecture for AWS VPC that involves all layers in a network. These security features also align security controls with the application requirement of scalability, availability, and performance.

Let's look at these security features in detail.

Security Groups

A security group is a virtual firewall to control ingress and egress traffic at the instance level for all instances in your VPC. Each VPC has its own default security group. When you launch an instance without assigning a security group, AWS will assign a default security group of VPC with this instance. Each instance can be assigned up to five security groups.

For a security group, in order to control ingress and egress traffic, we need to define rules for a security group. These rules need to be defined separately for controlling ingress and egress traffic. These rules are only permissive; that is, there can only be allow rules and there can't be deny rules.

When you create a new security group, by default, it does not allow any inbound traffic. You have to create a rule that allows inbound traffic. By default, a security group has a rule that allows all outbound traffic. Security groups are stateless, so if you create a rule for inbound traffic that allows traffic to flow in, this rule will allow outbound traffic as well; there is no need to create a separate rule to allow outbound traffic. These rules are editable and are applied immediately. You can add, modify, or delete a security group, and these changes are effective immediately as well. You can perform these actions from the AWS console or through the command line or an API.

An ENI can be associated with up to five security groups, while a security group can be associated with multiple instances. However, these instances cannot communicate with each other unless you configure rules in your security group to allow this. There is one exception to this behavior: the default security group already has these rules configured.

The following figure shows the security groups set up in my AWS account. This security group is created for the web server, so it has rules configured in order to allow HTTP and HTTPS traffic. It also allows SSH access on port 22 for logging into this instance:

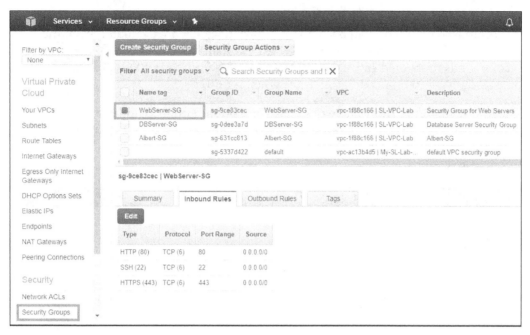

Figure 9: AWS VPC security groups

Network Access Control List

The **network access control list (NACL)**, as it is popularly known, is another virtual firewall provided by AWS VPC to configure inbound and outbound traffic for your subnets inside a VPC. So, all instances within this subnet are going to use the same configuration for inbound and outbound traffic. NACLs are used for creating guardrails in an organization for your network on the cloud as it does not offer granular control. Moreover, NACLs are usually configured by system administrators in an organization.

Every VPC has a default NACL that allows all inbound and outbound traffic by default. When you create a custom NACL, it denies all inbound and outbound traffic by default. Any subnet that is not explicitly associated with an NACL is associated with a default NACL and allows all traffic, so make sure all subnets in your VPCs are explicitly associated with an NACL.

NACL uses rules similar to security groups to configure inbound and outbound traffic for a subnet. Unlike security groups, NACL gives you the option to create allow and deny rules. NACL is stateless and you will need to create separate rules for inbound and outbound traffic.

Each subnet in your VPC can be attached to only one NACL. However, one NACL can be attached to more than one subnet. Rules in NACL are evaluated from the lower to the higher number, and the highest number you can have is 32776. AWS recommends that you create rules in multiples of 100, such as 100, 200, 300, and so on, so you have room to add more rules when required.

The following figure shows network ACL for a public subnet. It allows inbound and outbound HTTP and HTTPS traffic. This NACL can be used for all public subnets that will contain all instances that need to access the internet and those that are publicly accessible:

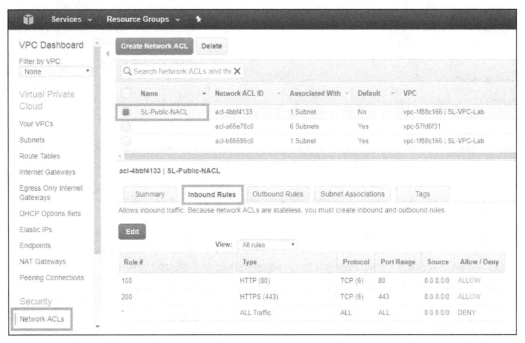

Figure 10: AWS VPC NACL

VPC Flow Logs

VPC facilitates the flow of inbound and outbound traffic for all resources in your VPC. It is important to monitor the flow of this IP traffic on a continuous basis in order to ensure that all traffic is going to the desired recipient and is received from expected resources. This feature is also useful for troubleshooting issues related to traffic not reaching its destination or vice versa. The VPC flow log is a very important security tool that helps monitor the security of your network in the AWS cloud.

You can create a flow log for your VPC as well as a subnet and a network interface based on your requirement. For a VPC flow log, all resources in VPC are monitored. For a subnet flow log, all resources in a subnet are monitored. This can take up to 15 minutes to collect data after you have created a flow log.

Each network interface has a unique log stream that is published to a log group in AWS CloudWatch logs. You can create multiple flow logs publishing data to one log. These logs streams consist of flow log records that are essentially log events with fields describing all the traffic for that resource. Log streams contain flow log records, which are log events consisting of fields that describe the traffic, such as the accepted traffic or rejected traffic for that network interface.

You can configure the type of traffic you want to monitor, including accepted, rejected, or all traffic for the flow log you create. You give this log a name in CloudWatch logs, where it will be published, and choose a resource you want to monitor. You will also need the **Amazon Resource Name** (**ARN**) of an IAM role that will be used to publish this flow log to CloudWatch logs group. These flow logs are not real-time log streams.

You can also create flow logs for network interfaces created by other AWS services, such as AWS RDS, AWS workspaces, and so on. However, these services cannot create flow logs; instead, you should use AWS EC2 to create flow logs, either from the AWS console or through the EC2 API. VPC flow logs are offered free of charge; you are charged only for logs. You can delete a flow log if you no longer need it. It might take several minutes before this deleted flow log stops collecting data for your network interface.

VPC flow logs have certain limitations. You cannot create VPC flow logs for peered VPCs that are not in your AWS account. VPC flow logs can't be tagged. A flow log cannot be modified after it is created; you need to delete this flow log and create another one with the required configuration. Flow logs do not capture all types of traffic, such as traffic generated by instances when they contact Amazon DNS servers, traffic to and from 169.254.169.254 for getting instance metadata, and so on.

VPC Access Control

As discussed in IAM, all AWS services require permission to access their resources. It is imperative to define access control for VPC as well. You need to grant appropriate permissions to all users, applications, and AWS services to access all VPC resources. You can define granular, resource-level permissions for VPC, which allows you to control what resources could be accessed or modified in your VPC.

You can give permissions such as managing a VPC, a read-only permission for VPC, or managing a specific resource for VPC, such as a security group or a network ACL.

Creating VPC

Let's look at steps to create a custom VPC in an AWS account. This VPC will be created using IPv4 **Classless Inter-Domain Routing (CIDR)** block. It will have one public subnet and one public facing instance in this subnet. It will also have one private subnet and one instance in private subnet. For instance, for a private subnet to access the internet, we will use a NAT gateway in a public subnet. This VPC will have security groups and network ACL configured to allow egress and ingress internet traffic along with routes configured to support this scenario:

1. Create a VPC with a /16 IPv4 CIDR block such as 10.0.0.0/16.

2. Create an internet gateway and attach it to this VPC.

3. Create one subnet with /24 IPv4 CIDR block, such as 10.0.0.0/24, and call it a public subnet. Note that this CIDR block is a subset of a VPC CIDR block.

4. Create another subnet with /24 IPv4 CIDR block, such as 10.0.1.0/24 and call it a private subnet. Note that this CIDR block is a subset of a VPC CIDR block and it does not overlap the CIDR block of a public subnet.

5. Create a custom route table and create a route for all traffic going to the internet to go through the internet gateway. Associate this route table with the public subnet.

6. Create a NAT gateway and associate it with the public subnet. Allocate one Elastic IP address and associate it with the NAT gateway.

7. Create a custom route in the main route table for all traffic going to the internet to go through NAT gateway. Associate this route table with the private subnet. This step will facilitate the routing of all internet traffic for instances in the private subnet to go through the NAT gateway. This will ensure IP addresses for private instances are not exposed to the internet.

8. Create a network ACL for each of these subnets. Configure rules that will define inbound and outbound traffic access for these subnets. Associate these NACLs with their respective subnets.

9. Create security groups for instances to be placed in public and private subnets. Configure rules for these security groups as per the access required. Assign these security groups with instances.

10. Create one instance each in the public and private subnet for this VPC. Assign a security group to each of them. An instance in a public subnet should have either a public IP or an EIP address.

11. Verify that the public instance can access the internet and private instances can access the internet through the NAT gateway.

Once all steps are completed, our newly created custom VPC will have the following architecture. Private instances are referred to as database servers and public instances are referred to as Web servers in the diagram. Note that the NAT gateway should have the Elastic IP address to send traffic to the internet gateway as the source IP address. This VPC has both the public and private subnet in one availability zone; however, in order to have a highly available and fault-tolerant architecture, you can have a similar configuration of resources in additional availability zones:

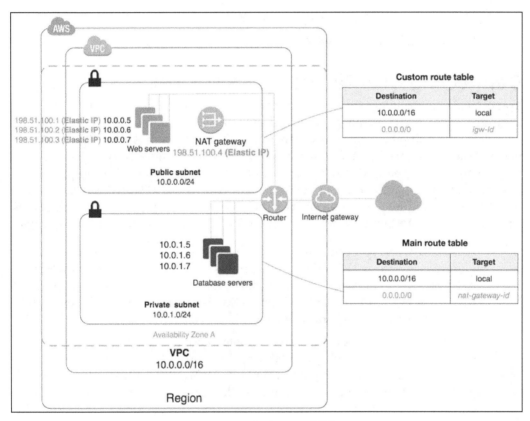

Figure 11: AWS custom VPC

VPC Connectivity Options

One of the major features of AWS VPC is the connectivity options it provides for securely connecting various networks with their AWS networks. In this section, you will learn about various connectivity options for AWS VPC, such as connecting remote customer networks with VPC, connecting multiple VPCs into a shared virtual network, and so on. We will look at three connectivity options in detail:

- Connecting the user network to AWS VPC
- Connecting AWS VPC with another AWS VPC
- Connecting the internal user with AWS VPC

Connecting User Network to AWS VPC

You can extend and integrate your resources in your remote networks, such as compute power, security, monitoring, and so on, by leveraging your resources in AWS VPC. By doing this, your users can access all resources in AWS VPC seamlessly like any other resource in internal networks. This type of connectivity requires you to have non-overlapping IP ranges for your networks on the cloud and on-premises, so ensure that you have a unique CIDR block for your AWS VPC. AWS recommends that you use a unique, single, non-overlapping, and contiguous CIDR block for every VPC. You can connect your network with AWS VPC securely in the following ways:

- **HardwareVPN**: You can configure AWS-compatible customer VPN gateways to access AWS VPC over an industry standard, encrypted IPSec hardware VPN connection. You are billed for each VPN connection hour, that is, for every hour your VPC connection is up and running. Along with it, you are charged for data transfer as well.

  This option is easier to configure and install and uses an existing internet connection. It is also highly available as AWS provides two VPN tunnels in an active and standby mode by default. AWS provides virtual private gateway with two endpoints for automatic failover. You need to configure, customer gateway side of this VPN connection, this customer gateway could be software or hardware in your remote network.

  On the flip side, hardware VPN connections have data transfer speed limitation. Since they use an internet to establish connectivity, the performance of this connection, including network latency and availability, is dependent on the internet condition.

- **Direct connect**: You can connect your AWS VPC to your remote network using a dedicated network connection provided by AWS authorized partners over 1-gigabit or 10-gigabit Ethernet fiber-optic cable. One end of this cable is connected to your router, the other to an AWS Direct Connect router. You get improved, predictable network performance with reduced bandwidth cost. With direct connect, you can bypass the internet and connect directly to your resources in AWS, including AWS VPC.

  You can pair direct connect with a hardware VPN connection for a redundant, highly available connectivity between your remote networks and AWS VPC. The following diagram shows the AWS direct connect service interfacing with your remote network:

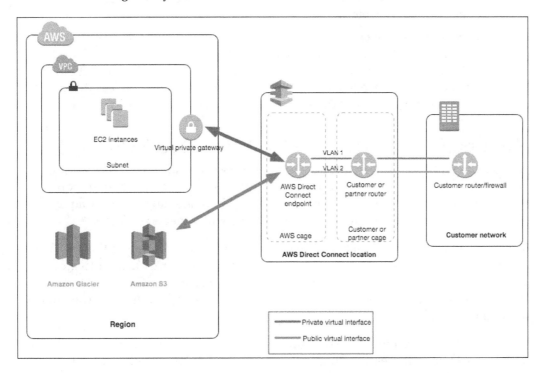

Figure 12: AWS direct connect

- **AWS VPN CloudHub**: You might have multiple remote networks that need to connect securely with AWS VPC. For such scenarios, you will create multiple VPN connections, and you will use AWS VPN CloudHub to provide secure communication between these sites. This is a hub and spoke model that can be used either for primary connectivity or as a backup option. It uses existing internet connections and VPN connections.

You create a virtual private gateway for your VPC with multiple customer gateways for your remote networks to use AWS VPN CloudHub. These remote networks should not have overlapping IP networks. The pricing model for this option is similar to that of a hardware VPN connection.

- **SoftwareVPN**: Instead of a hardware VPN connection, you can also use an EC2 instance in your VPC with a software VPN appliance running in order to connect your remote network. AWS does not provide any software VPN appliance; however, you can use software VPN appliances through a range of products provided by AWS partners and various open source communities present on AWS marketplace. It also uses the internet for connectivity; hence, reliability, availability, and network performance are dependent on the internet speed.

This option, however, supports a wide variety of VPN vendors, products, and protocols. It is completely managed by customers. It is helpful for scenarios where you are required to manage both ends of a connection, either for compliance purposes or if you are using connectivity devices that are currently not supported by AWS.

Connecting AWS VPC with Other AWS VPC

If you have multiple VPCs in multiple regions across the globe, you may want to connect these VPCs to create a larger, secure network. This connectivity option works only if your VPCs do not have overlapping IP ranges and have a unique CIDR block. Let's look at the ways to connect AWS VPC with other AWS VPCs.

You can connect two VPCs in the same region using a VPC peering option in AWS VPC. Resources in these VPCs can communicate with each other using private IP addresses as if they are in the same network. You can have a VPC peering connection with a VPC in your AWS account and VPC in other AWS accounts as long as they are in the same region.

AWS uses its own existing infrastructure for this connection. It is not a gateway or a VPN connection that uses any physical device. It is not a single point of failure or a network performance bottleneck.

VPC peering is the most preferred method of connecting AWS VPCs. It is suited for many scenarios for large and small organizations. Let's look at some of the most common scenarios.

If you need to provide full access to resources across two or more VPCs, you can do that by peering them. For example, you have multiple branch offices in various regions across the globe and each branch office has a different VPC. Your headquarter needs to access all resources for all VPCs for all your branch offices. You can accomplish this by creating a VPC in each region and peering all other VPCs with your VPC.

You might have a centralized VPC that contains information required by other VPCs in your organization, such as policies related to human resources. This is a read-only VPC and you would not want to provide full access to resources in this VPC. You can create VPC peering connection and restrict access for this centralized VPC.

You can also have a centralized VPC that might be shared with your customers. Each customer can peer their VPC with your centralized VPC, but they cannot access resources in other customers' VPC.

Data transfer charges for a VPC peering connection are similar to charges for data transfer across availability zones. As discussed, VPC peering is limited to VPCs in the same region. A VPC peering is a one-to-one connection between two VPCs; transitive peering is not allowed for a peering connection. In the following diagram, VPC A is peered with VPC B and VPC C; however, VPC B is not peered with VPC C implicitly. It has to be peered explicitly:

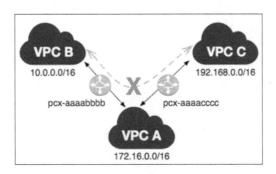

Figure 13: AWS VPC Transitive Peering

Apart from VPC peering, there are other options for connecting VPCs, such as software VPN, hardware VPN, and AWS direct connect as well. All of these options have benefits and limitations similar to the one discussed in the previous section.

Connecting Internal User with AWS VPC

If you want to allow your internal users to access resources in AWS VPC, you can leverage your existing remote networks to AWS VPC connections using either hardware VPN, direct connect, or software VPN depending on your requirement. Alternatively, you can combine these connectivity options to suit your requirements, such as cost, speed, reliability, availability, and so on.

VPC Limits

AWS VPC has limits for various components in a region. Most of these are soft limits and can be increased by contacting AWS support from the AWS console and submitting a request by filling the Amazon VPC limits form available in the AWS console.

Let's look at these limits:

Resource	Default limit
VPCs per region	5
Subnets per VPC	200
Elastic IP addresses per region	5
Flow logs per resource in a region	2
Customer gateways per region	50
Internet gateways per region	5
NAT gateways per availability zone	5
Virtual private gateways per region	5
Network ACLs per VPC	200
Rules per network ACL	20
Network interfaces per region	350
Route tables per VPC	200
Routes per route table	50
Security groups per VPC (per region)	500
Rules per security group	50
Security groups per network interface	5
Active VPC peering connections per VPC	50
VPC endpoints per region	20
VPN connections per region	50
VPN connections per VPC (per virtual private gateway)	10

Table 1: AWS VPC limit

VPC Best Practices

In this section, we will go through an exhaustive list of best practices to be followed for AWS VPC. Most of these are recommended by AWS as well. Implementing these best practices will ensure that your resources, including your servers, data, and applications, are integrated with other AWS services and secured in AWS VPC. Remember that VPC is not a typical data center and it should not be treated as one.

Plan Your VPC before You Create It

Always start by planning and designing architecture for your VPC before you create it. A bad VPC design will have serious implications on the flexibility, scalability, availability, and security of your infrastructure. So, spend a good amount of time planning out your VPC before you actually start creating it.

Start with the objective of creating a VPC: is it for one application or for a business unit? Spec out all subnets you will need and figure out your availability and fault-tolerance requirements. Find out what all connectivity options you will need for connecting all internal and external networks. You might need to plan for a number of VPCs if you need to connect with networks in more than one region.

Choose the Highest CIDR Block

Once you create VPC with a CIDR block, you cannot change it. You will have to create another VPC and migrate your resources to a new VPC if you want to change your CIDR block. So, take a good look at your current resources and your requirements for the next few years in order to plan and design your VPC architecture. A VPC can have a CIDR block ranging from /16 to /28, which means you can have between 65,536 and 16 IP addresses for your VPC. AWS recommends that you choose the highest CIDR block available, so always go for /16 CIDR block for your VPC. This way, you won't be short of IP addresses if you need to increase your instances exponentially.

Unique IP Address Range

All VPC connectivity options require you to have non-overlapping IP ranges. Consider future connectivity to all your internal and external networks. Make sure you take note of all available IP ranges for all your environments, including remote networks, data centers, offices, other AWS VPCs, and so on, before you assign CIDR ranges for your VPC. None of these should conflict and overlap with any network that you want to connect with.

Leave the Default VPC Alone

AWS provides a default VPC in every region for your AWS account. It is best to leave this VPC alone and start with a custom VPC for your requirement. The default VPC has all components associated with it; however, the security configuration of all these components, such as subnets, security groups, and network ACLs are quite open to the world. There is no private subnet either. So, it is a good idea to create your own VPC from scratch using either a VPC wizard in the AWS console or creating it manually through the AWS console or AWS CLI. You can configure all resources as per your requirement for your custom VPC.

Moreover, by default, if a subnet is not associated with a route table or an NACL, it is associated with the main route table and default NACL. These two components don't have any restrictions on inbound and outbound traffic, and you risk exposing your resources to the entire world.

You should not modify the main route table either; doing that might give other subnets routes that they shouldn't be given. Always create a custom route table and keep the main route table as it is.

Design for Region Expansion

AWS keeps on expanding its regions by adding more availability zones to them. We know that one subnet cannot span more than one availability zone, and distributing our resources across availability zones makes our application highly available and fault-tolerant. It is a good idea to reserve some IP address for future expansion while creating subnets with a subset of VPC CIDR block. By default, AWS reserves five IP address in every subnet for internal usage; make a note of this while allocating IP addresses to a subnet.

Tier Your Subnets

Ideally, you should design your subnets according to your architecture tiers, such as the database tier, the application tier, the business tier, and so on, based on their routing needs, such as public subnets needing a route to the internet gateway, and so on. You should also create multiple subnets in as many availability zones as possible to improve your fault-tolerance. Each availability zone should have identically sized subnets, and each of these subnets should use a routing table designed for them depending on their routing need. Distribute your address space evenly across availability zones and keep the reserved space for future expansion.

Follow the Least Privilege Principle

For every resource you provision or configure in your VPC, follow the least privilege principle. So, if a subnet has resources that do not need to access the internet, it should be a private subnet and should have routing based on this requirement. Similarly, security groups and NACLs should have rules based on this principle. They should allow access only for traffic required. Do not add a route to the internet gateway to the main route table as it is the default route table for all subnets.

Keep Most Resources in the Private Subnet

In order to keep your VPC and resources in your VPC secure, ensure that most of the resources are inside a private subnet by default. If you have instances that need to communicate with the internet, then you should add an **Elastic Load Balancer** (ELB) in the public subnet and add all instances behind this ELB in the private subnet.

Use NAT devices (a NAT instance or a NAT gateway) to access public networks from your private subnet. AWS recommends that you use a NAT gateway over a NAT instance as the NAT gateway is a fully managed, highly available, and redundant component.

Creating VPCs for Different Use Cases

You should ideally create one VPC each for your development, testing, and production environments. This will secure your resources from keeping them separate from each other, and it will also reduce your blast radius, that is, the impact on your environment if one of your VPCs goes down.

For most use cases such as application isolation, multi-tenant application, and business unit alignment, it is a good idea to create a separate VPC.

Favor Security Groups over NACLs

Security groups and NACLs are virtual firewalls available for configuring security rules for your instances and subnets respectively. While security groups are easier to configure and manage, NACLs are different. It is recommended that NACLs be used sparingly and not be changed often. NACLs should be the security policy for your organization as it does not work at a granular level. NACL rules are tied to the IP address and for a subnet, with the addition of every single rule, the complexity and management of these rules becomes exponentially difficult.

Security group rules are tied to instances and these rules span the entire VPC; they are stateful and dynamic in nature. They are easier to manage and should be kept simple. Moreover, security groups can pass other security groups as an object reference in order to allow access, so you can allow access to your database server security group only for the application server security group.

IAM Your VPC

Access control for your VPC should be on top of your list while creating a VPC. You can configure IAM roles for your instances and assign them at any point. You can provide granular access for provisioning new resources inside a VPC and reduce the blast radius by restricting access to high-impact components such as various connectivity options, NACL configuration, subnet creation, and so on.

There will usually be more than one person managing all resources for your VPC; you should assign permissions to these people based on their role and by following the principle of least privileges. If someone does not need access to a resource, that access shouldn't be given in the first place.

Periodically, use the access advisor function available in IAM to find out whether all the permissions are being used as expected and take necessary actions based on your findings.

Create an IAM VPC admin group to manage your VPC and its resources.

Using VPC Peering

Use VPC peering whenever possible. When you connect two VPCs using the VPC peering option, instances in these VPCs can communicate with each other using a private IP address. For a VPC peering connection, AWS uses its own network and you do not have to rely on an external network for the performance of your connection, and it is a lot more secure.

Using Elastic IP Instead of Public IP

Always use **Elastic IP** (**EIP**) instead of public IP for all resources that need to connect to the internet. The EIPs are associated with an AWS account instead of an instance. They can be assigned to an instance in any state, whether the instance is running or whether it is stopped. It persists without an instance so you can have high availability for your application depending on an IP address. The EIP can be reassigned and moved to **Elastic Network Interface** (**ENI**) as well. Since these IPs don't change, they can be whitelisted by target resources.

All these advantages of EIP over a public IP make it more favorable when compared with a public IP.

Tagging in VPC

Always tag your resources in a VPC. The tagging strategy should be part of your planning phase. A good practice is to tag a resource immediately after it is created. Some common tags include version, owner, team, project code, cost center, and so on. Tags are supported by AWS billing and for resource-level permissions.

Monitoring a VPC

Monitoring is imperative to the security of any network, such as AWS VPC. Enable AWS CloudTrail and VPC flow logs to monitor all activities and traffic movement. The AWS CloudTrail will record all activities, such as provisioning, configuring, and modifying all VPC components. The VPC flow log will record all the data flowing in and out of the VPC for all the resources in VPC. Additionally, you can set up config rules for the AWS Config service for your VPC for all resources that should not have changes in their configuration.

Connect these logs and rules with AWS CloudWatch to notify you of anything that is not expected behavior and control changes within your VPC. Identify irregularities within your network, such as resources receiving unexpected traffic in your VPC, adding instances in the VPC with configuration not approved by your organization, among others.

Similarly, if you have unused resources lying in your VPC, such as security groups, EIP, gateways, and so on, remove them by automating the monitoring of these resources.

Lastly, you can use third-party solutions available on AWS marketplace for monitoring your VPC. These solutions integrate with existing AWS monitoring solutions, such as AWS CloudWatch, AWS CloudTrail, and so on, and provide information in a user-friendly way in the form of dashboards.

Summary

The VPC is responsible for securing your network, including your infrastructure on the cloud, and that makes this AWS service extremely critical for mastering security in AWS. In this lesson, you learned the basics of VPC, including features, benefits, and most common use cases.

We went through the various components of VPC and you learned how to configure all of them to create a custom VPC. Alongside, we looked at components that make VPC secure, such as routing, security groups, and so on.

We also looked at multiple connectivity options, such as a private, shared, or dedicated connection provided by VPC. These connectivity options enable us to create a hybrid cloud environment, a large connected internal network for your organization, and many such secure, highly available environments to address many more scenarios.

Lastly, you learned about the limits of various VPC components and we looked at an exhaustive list of VPC best practices.

In the next lesson, we will look at ways to secure data in AWS: data security in AWS in a nutshell. You will learn about encrypting data in transit and at rest. We will also look at securing data using various AWS services.

Assessments

1. Which among the following is used for separating resources, such as web servers and database servers?

    1. Subnets

    2. Route tables

    3. Elastic Network Interfaces

    4. NAT

2. State whether the following statement is True or False: By default, every VPC has a network interface attached to every instance.

3. One route table can be attached to multiple _____.

    1. VPC

    2. Subnets

    3. NAT

    4. Elastic Network Interfaces

4. How to access private subnets publicly?

5. _____ can be associated with up to five security groups.

    1. ENI

    2. NAT

    3. VPC

    4. Route tables

2
Data Security in AWS

Data security in the AWS platform can be classified into two broad categories:

- Protecting data at rest
- Protecting data in transit

Furthermore, data security has the following components that help in securing data in multiple ways:

- Data encryption
- **Key Management Services (KMS)**
- Access control
- AWS service security features

AWS provides you with various tools and services to secure your data in AWS when your data is in transit or when your data is at rest. These tools and services include resource access control using AWS **Identity and Access Management (IAM)**, data encryption, and managed KMS, such as AWS KMS for creating and controlling keys used for data encryption. The AWS KMS provides multiple options for managing your entire **Key Management Infrastructure (KMI)**. Alternatively, you also have the option to go with the fully managed AWS CloudHSM service, a cloud-based **hardware security module (HSM)** that helps you generate and use your own keys for encryption purpose.

AWS recently launched a new security service to protect your sensitive data by using machine learning algorithms; this service is called Amazon Macie. As of now, it offers security for all data stored in your Amazon **Simple Storage Service (S3)**.

If you want to protect your data further due to business or regulatory compliance purposes, you can enable additional features for accidental deletion of data such as the versioning feature in AWS S3, MFA for accessing and deleting data, enable cross-region replication for more than one copy of your data in AWS S3, and so on.

All data storage and data processing AWS services provide multiple features to secure your data. Such features include data encryption at rest, data encryption in transit, MFA for access control and for deletion of data, versioning for accidental data deletion, granular access control and authorization policies, cross-region replication, and so on.

Introduction

In this lesson, we will learn about protecting data in the AWS platform for various AWS services. To begin with, we will go over the fundamentals of encryption and decryption and how encryption and decryption of data work in AWS. Post that, we will start with security features for securing data in transit and at rest for each of the following AWS services:

- Amazon Simple Storage Service (S3)
- Amazon Elastic Block Storage (EBS)
- Amazon Relational Database Service (RDS)
- Amazon Glacier
- Amazon DynamoDB
- Amazon Elastic Map Reduce (EMR)

We will look at data encryption in AWS and we will learn about three models that are available for managing keys for encryption and how we can use these models for encrypting data in various AWS services such as, AWS S3, Amazon EBS, AWS Storage Gateway, Amazon RDS, and so on.

Next, we will deep dive on AWS KMS and go through KMS features and major KMS components.

Furthermore, we will go through the AWS CloudHSM service with its benefits and popular use cases.

Lastly, we will take a look at Amazon Macie, the newest security service launched by AWS to protect sensitive data using machine learning at the backend.

Encryption and Decryption Fundamentals

Encryption of data can be defined as converting data known as plaintext into code, often known as **ciphertext** that is unreadable by anyone except the intended audience. Data encryption is the most popular way of adding another layer of security for preventing unauthorized access and use of data. Encryption is a two-step process: in the first step, data is encrypted using a combination of an encryption key and an encryption algorithm, in the second step, data is decrypted using a combination of a decryption key and a decryption algorithm to view data in its original form.

The following three components are required for encryption. These three components work hand in hand for securing your data.

- Data to be encrypted
- Algorithm for encryption
- Encryption keys to be used alongside the data and the algorithm

There are two types of encryption available, symmetric and asymmetric. Asymmetric encryption is also known as public key encryption. Symmetric encryption uses the same secret key to perform both the encryption and decryption processes. On the other hand, asymmetric encryption uses two keys, a public key for encryption and a corresponding private key for decryption, making this option more secure and at the same time more difficult to maintain as you would need to manage two separate keys for encryption and decryption.

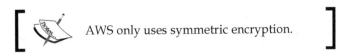 AWS only uses symmetric encryption.

For encrypting data in AWS, the plaintext data key is used to convert plaintext data into ciphertext using the encryption algorithm. The following figure shows a typical workflow of the data encryption process in AWS:

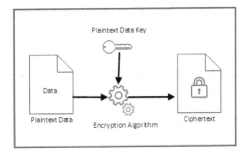

Figure 1: AWS encryption workflow

Decryption converts the encrypted data (ciphertext) into plaintext, essentially reversing the encryption process. For decrypting data in AWS, ciphertext uses the plaintext data key for converting ciphertext into plaintext by applying the decryption algorithm. The following figure shows the AWS decryption workflow for converting ciphertext into plaintext:

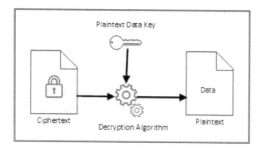

Figure 2: AWS decryption workflow

Envelope Encryption

AWS uses envelope encryption, a process to encrypt data directly. This process provides a balance between the process and security for encrypting your data. This process has the following steps for encrypting and storing your data:

1. The AWS service being used for encryption will generate a data key when a user requests data to be encrypted.

2. This data key is used to encrypt data along with the encryption algorithm.

3. Once the data is encrypted, the data key is encrypted as well by using the key-encrypting key that is unique to the AWS service used to store your data such, as AWS S3.

4. This encrypted data and encrypted data key are stored in the AWS storage service.

   Note that the key-encrypting key also known as **master key** is stored and managed separately from the data and the data key itself. When decrypted data is required to be converted to plaintext data, the preceding mentioned process is reversed.

The following figure depicts the end-to-end workflow for the envelope encryption process; the master key in the following figure is the key-encrypting key:

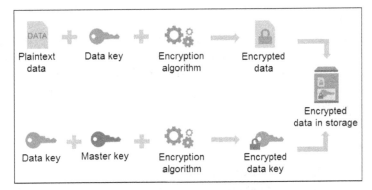

Figure 3: AWS envelope encryption

Securing Data at Rest

You might be required to encrypt your data at rest for all AWS services or for some of the AWS storage services depending on your organizational policies, industry or government regulations, compliance, or simply for adding another layer of security for your data. AWS provides several options for encrypting data at rest including fully automated and fully managed AWS encryption solutions, manual encryption solutions, client-side encryption, and so on. In this section, we are going to go over these options for each AWS storage service.

Amazon S3

The S3 is one of the major and most commonly used storage services in the AWS platform. It supports a wide range of use cases such as file storage, archival records, disaster recovery, website hosting, and so on. The S3 provides multiple features to protect your data such as encryption, MFA, versioning, access control policies, cross-region replication, and so on. Let us look at these features for protecting your data at rest in S3.

Permissions

The S3 gives you an option to add bucket level and object level permissions in addition to the IAM policies for better access control. These permissions allow you to control information theft, data integrity, unauthorized access, and deletion of your data.

Versioning

The S3 has a versioning feature that maintains all versions of objects that are modified or deleted in a bucket. Versioning prevents accidental deletion and overwrites for all your objects. You can restore an object to its previous version if it is compromised. Versioning is disabled by default. Once versioning is enabled for a bucket, it can only be suspended. It cannot be disabled.

Replication

In order to provide the 11 9s of durability (99.999999999), S3 replicates each object stored across all availability zones within the respective region. This process ensures data availability in the event of a disaster by maintaining multiple copies of your data within a region. The S3 also offers a cross region replication feature that is used to automatically and asynchronously replicate objects stored in your bucket from one region to an S3 bucket in another region. This bucket level feature can be used to back up your s3 objects across regions.

Server-Side Encryption

The S3 provides server-side encryption feature for encrypting user data. This encryption process is transparent to the end user (client) as it is performed at the server side. AWS manages the master key used for this encryption and ensures that this key is rotated on a regular basis. AWS generates a unique encryption key for each object and then encrypts the object using AES-256. The encryption key then encrypts itself using AES-256, with a master key that is stored in a secure location.

Client-Side Encryption

The AWS also supports client-side encryption where encryption keys are created and managed by you. Data is encrypted by your applications before it is submitted to AWS for storage and the data is decrypted after it is received from the AWS services. The data is stored in the AWS service in an encrypted form and AWS has no knowledge of encryption algorithms or keys used to encrypt this data. You can also use either symmetric or asymmetric keys along with any encryption algorithm for client-side encryption. AWS provided Java SDK, offers client-side encryption features for Amazon S3.

Amazon EBS

Amazon EBS is an abstract block storage service providing persistent block level storage volumes. These volumes are attached to Amazon **Elastic Compute Cloud (EC2)** instances. Each of these volumes is automatically replicated within its availability zone that protects against component failure of an EBS volume. Let us look at options available to protect data at rest, stored in EBS volumes that are attached to an EC2 instance.

Replication

AWS stores each EBS volume as a file and creates two copies of this volume in the same availability zone. This replication process provides redundancy against hardware failure. However, for the purpose of disaster recovery, AWS recommends replicating data at the application level.

Backup

You can create snapshots for your EBS volumes to get point in time copies of your data stored in EBS volume. These snapshots are stored in AWS S3 so they provide the same durability as any other object stored in S3. If an EBS volume is corrupt or if data is modified or deleted from an EBS volume, you can use snapshots to restore the data to its desired state. You can authorize access for these snapshots through IAM as well. These EBS snapshots are AWS objects to which you can assign permissions for your IAM identities such as users, groups, and roles.

Encryption

You can encrypt data in your EBS volumes using AWS native encryption features such as AWS KMS. When you create a snapshot of an encrypted volume, you get an encrypted snapshot. You can use these encrypted EBS volume to store your data securely at rest and attach these to your EC2 instances.

The **Input Output Per Second (IOPS)** performance of an encrypted volume is similar to an unencrypted volume, with negligible effect on latency. Moreover, an encrypted volume can be accessed in a similar way as an unencrypted volume. One of the best parts about encrypting EBS volume is that both encryption and decryption require no additional action from the user, EC2 instance, or the user's application, and they are handled transparently.

Snapshots of encrypted volumes are automatically encrypted. Volumes created using these encrypted snapshots are also automatically encrypted.

Amazon RDS

Amazon RDS enables you to encrypt your data for EBS volumes, snapshots, read replicas and automated backups of your RDS instances. One of the benefits of working with RDS is that you do not have to write any decryption algorithm to decrypt your encrypted data stored in RDS. This process of decryption is handled by Amazon RDS.

Amazon Glacier

AWS uses AES-256 for encrypting each Amazon Glacier archive and generates separate unique encryption keys for each of these archives. By default, all data stored on Amazon Glacier is protected using the server-side encryption. The encryption key is then encrypted itself by using the AES-256 with a master key. This master key is rotated regularly and stored in a secure location.

Additionally, you can encrypt data prior to uploading it to the Amazon Glacier if you want more security for your data at rest.

Amazon DynamoDB

Amazon DynamoDB can be used without adding protection. However, for additional protection, you can also implement a data encryption layer over the standard DynamoDB service. DynamoDB supports number, string, and raw binary data type formats. When storing encrypted fields in DynamoDB, it is a best practice to use raw binary fields or Base64-encoded string fields.

Amazon EMR

Amazon EMR is a managed **Hadoop Framework** service in the cloud. AWS provides the AMIs for Amazon EMR, and you can't use custom AMIs or your own EBS volumes.

Amazon EMR automatically configures Amazon EC2 firewall settings such as network **access control list** (**ACL**) and security groups for controlling network access for instances. These EMR clusters are launched in an Amazon **Virtual Private Cloud** (**VPC**).

By default, Amazon EMR instances do not encrypt data at rest. Usually, EMR clusters store data in S3 or in DynamoDB for persistent data. This data can be secured using the security options for these Amazon services as mentioned in the earlier sections.

Securing Data in Transit

Most of the web applications that are hosted on AWS will be sending data over the internet and it is imperative to protect data in transit. This transit will involve network traffic between clients and servers, and network traffic between servers. So data in transit needs to be protected at the network layer and the session layer.

AWS services provide IPSec and SSL/TLS support for securing data in transit. An IPSec protocol extends the IP protocol stack primarily for the network layer and allows applications on the upper layers to communicate securely without modification. The SSL/TLS, however, operates at the session layer.

The **Transport Layer Security (TLS)** is a standard set of protocols for securing communications over a network. TLS has evolved from **Secure Sockets Layer (SSL)** and is considered to be a more refined system.

Let us look at options to secure network traffic in AWS for various AWS services.

Amazon S3

The AWS S3 supports the SSL/TLS protocol for encrypting data in transit by default. All data requests in AWS S3 is accessed using HTTPS. This includes AWS S3 service management requests such as saving an object to an S3 bucket, user payload such as content and the metadata of objects saved, modified, or fetched from S3 buckets.

You can access S3 using either the AWS Management Console or through S3 APIs.

When you access S3 through AWS Management Console, a secure SSL/TLS connection is established between the service console endpoint and the client browser. This connection secures all subsequent traffic for this session.

When you access S3 through S3 APIs that is through programs, an SSL/TLS connection is established between the AWS S3 endpoint and client. This secure connection then encapsulates all requests and responses within this session.

Amazon RDS

You have an option to connect to the AWS RDS service through your AWS EC2 instance within the same region. If you use this option, you can use the existing security of the AWS network and rely on it. However, if you are connecting to AWS RDS using the internet, you'll need additional protection in the form of TLS/SSL.

As of now SSL/TLS is currently supported by AWS RDS MySQL and Microsoft SQL instance connections only.

AWS RDS for Oracle native network encryption encrypts the data in transit. It helps you to encrypt network traffic traveling over Oracle Net services.

Amazon DynamoDB

You can connect to AWS DynamoDB using other AWS services in the same region and while doing so, you can use the existing security of AWS network and rely on it. However, while accessing AWS DynamoDB from the internet, you might want to use HTTP over SSL/TLS (HTTPS) for enhanced security. AWS advises users to avoid HTTP access for all connections over the internet for AWS DynamoDB and other AWS services.

Amazon EMR

Amazon EMR offers several encryption options for securing data in transit. These options are open source features, application specific, and vary by EMR version.

For traffic between Hadoop nodes, no additional security is usually required as all nodes reside in the same availability zone for Amazon EMR. These nodes are secured by the AWS standard security measures at the physical and infrastructure layer.

For traffic between Hadoop cluster and Amazon S3, Amazon EMR uses HTTPS for sending data between EC2 and S3. It uses HTTPS by default for sending data between the Hadoop cluster and the Amazon DynamoDB as well.

For traffic between users or applications interacting with the Hadoop cluster, it is advisable to use SSH or REST protocols for interactive access to applications. You can also use Thrift or Avro protocols along with SSL/TLS.

For managing a Hadoop cluster, you would need to access the EMR master node. You should use SSH to access the EMR master node for administrative tasks and for managing the Hadoop cluster.

AWS KMS

AWS KMS is a fully managed service that supports encryption for your data at rest and data in transit while working with AWS services. AWS KMS lets you create and manage keys that are used to encrypt your data. It provides a fully managed and highly available key storage, management and auditing solution that can be used to encrypt data across AWS services as well as to encrypt data within your applications. It is low cost as default keys are stored in your account at no charge – you pay for key usage and for creating any additional master keys.

KMS Benefits

AWS KMS has various benefits such as importing your own keys in KMS and creating keys with aliases and description. You can disable keys temporarily and re-enable them. You can also delete keys that are no longer required or used. You can rotate your keys periodically or let AWS rotate them annually. Let us look at some major benefits of KMS in detail:

Fully Managed

AWS KMS is a fully managed service, where AWS takes care of underlying infrastructure to support high availability as it is deployed in multiple availability zones within a region, automatic scalability, security, and zero maintenance for the user. This allows the user to focus on the encryption requirement for their workload. AWS KMS provides 99.999999999% durability for your encrypted keys by storing multiple copies of these keys.

Centralized Key Management

AWS KMS gives you centralized control of all of your encryption keys. You can access KMS through the AWS Management Console, CLI, and AWS SDK for creating, importing, and rotating keys. You can also set up usage policies and audit KMS for key usage from any of these options for accessing AWS KMS.

Integration with AWS Services

AWS KMS integrates seamlessly with multiple AWS services to enable encryption of data stored in these AWS services such as S3, RDS, EMR, and so on. AWS KMS also integrates with management services, such as AWS CloudTrail, to log usage of each key, every single time it is used for audit purpose. It also integrates with IAM to provide access control.

Secure and Compliant

The AWS KMS is a secure service that ensures your master keys are not shared with anyone else. It uses hardened systems and hardening techniques to protect your unencrypted master keys. KMS keys are never transmitted outside of the AWS regions in which they were created. You can define which users can use keys and have granular permissions for accessing KMS.

The AWS KMS is compliant with many leading regulatory compliance schemes such as PCI-DSS Level 1, SOC1, SOC2, SOC3, ISO 9001, and so on.

KMS Components

Let us look at the important components of AWS KMS and understand how they work together to secure data in AWS. The envelope encryption is one of the key components of KMS that we discussed earlier in this lesson.

Customer Master Key (CMK)

The CMK is a primary component of KMS. These keys could be managed either by the customer or by AWS. You would usually need CMKs to protect your data keys (keys used for encrypting data). Each of these keys can be used to protect 4 KB of data directly. These CMKs are always encrypted when they leave AWS. For every AWS service that integrates with AWS KMS, AWS provides a CMK that is managed by AWS. This CMK is unique to your AWS account and region in which it is used.

Data Keys

Data keys are used to encrypt data. This data could be in your application outside of AWS. AWS KMS can be used to generate, encrypt, and decrypt data keys. However, AWS KMS does not store, manage, or track your data keys. These functions should be performed by you in your application.

Key Policies

A key policy is a document that contains permission for accessing CMK. You can decide who can use and manage CMK for all CMK that you create, and you can add this information to the key policy. This key policy can be edited to add, modify, or delete permissions for a customer managed CMK; however, a key policy for an AWS managed CMK cannot be edited.

Auditing CMK Usage

AWS KMS integrates with AWS CloudTrail to provide an audit trail of your key usage. You can save this trail that is generated as a log file in a S3 bucket. These log files contain information about all AWS KMS API requests made in the AWS Management Console, AWS SDKs, command line tools such as AWS CLI and all requests made through other AWS services that are integrated with AWS KMS. These log files will tell you about KMS operation, the identity of a requester along with the IP address, time of usage, and so on.

You can monitor, control, and investigate your key usage through AWS CloudTrail.

Key Management Infrastructure (KMI)

AWS KMS provides a secure KMI as a service to you. While encrypting and decrypting data, it is the responsibility of the KMI provider to keep your keys secure, and AWS KMS helps you keep your keys secure. The KMS is a managed service so you don't have to worry about scaling your infrastructure when your encryption requirement is increasing.

AWS CloudHSM

AWS and AWS partners offer various options such as AWS KMS to protect your data in AWS. However, due to contractual, regulatory compliance, or corporate requirements for security of an application or sensitive data, you might need additional protection. AWS CloudHSM is a cloud-based dedicated, single-tenant HSM allowing you to include secure key storage and high-performance crypto operations to your applications on the AWS platform. It enables you to securely generate, store, manage, and protect encryption keys in a way that these keys are accessible only by you or authorized users that only you specify and no one else.

AWS CloudHSM is a fully managed service that takes care of administrative, time-consuming tasks such as backups, software updates, hardware provisioning, and high availability by automating these tasks. However, AWS does not have any access to configure, create, manage, or use your CloudHSM. You can quickly scale by adding or removing HSM capacity on-demand with no upfront costs.

An HSM is a hardware device providing secure key storage and cryptographic operations inside a tamper-proof hardware appliance.

AWS CloudHSM runs in your VPC, as shown in the following figure, so it is secure by design as all VPC security features are available to secure your CloudHSM.

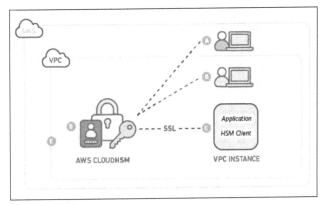

Figure 4: AWS CloudHSM

CloudHSM Features

Let us look at some features of the AWS CloudHSM service.

Generate and Use Encryption Keys Using HSMs

AWS CloudHSM provides FIPS 140-2 level 3 compliant HSM for using and generating your encryption keys. It protects your encryption keys with a single tenant, exclusive access, and dedicated tamper-proof device in your own AWS VPC.

Pay as You Go Model

AWS CloudHSM offers a utility pricing model like many other AWS services. You pay only for what you use and there are no upfront costs whatsoever. You are billed for every running hour (or partial hour) for every HSM you provision within a CloudHSM cluster.

Easy to Manage

AWS CloudHSM is a fully managed service, so you need not worry about scalability, high availability, hardware provisioning, or software patching. These tasks are taken care by of AWS. The AWS also takes automated encrypted backups of your HSM on a daily basis.

AWS monitors health and network availability of HSMs. It does not have access to keys stored inside these HSMs. This access is available only to you and users authorized by you. You are responsible for keys and cryptography operations. This separation of duties and role-based access control is inherent to CloudHSM design, as shown in the following figure:

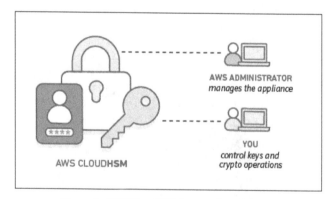

Figure 5: AWS CloudHSM separation of duties

AWS CloudHSM Use Cases

A CloudHSM cluster can store up to 3,500 keys of any type or size. It integrates with AWS CloudTrail so all activities related to CloudHSM are logged and you can get a history of all AWS API calls made to CloudHSM.

With so many features and benefits, AWS CloudHSM has many use cases when it comes to securing your data. Let us look at some of the most popular use cases for this service.

Offload SSL/TLS Processing for Web Servers

Web servers and web browsers often use SSL or TLS for a secure connection to transfer data over the internet. This connection requires the web server to use a public-private key pair along with a public key certificate in order to establish an HTTPS session with each client. This activity acts as an overhead for the web server in terms of additional computation. CloudHSM can help you offload this overhead by storing the web server's private key in HSM as it is designed for this purpose. This process is often known as SSL acceleration.

Protect Private Keys for an Issuing Certificate Authority

A certificate authority is an entity entrusted for issuing digital certificates for a public key infrastructure. These digital certificates are used by an individual or an organization for various scenarios by binding public keys to an identity. You need to protect private keys that are used to sign the certificates used by your certificate authority. CloudHSM can perform these cryptographic operations and store these private keys issued by your certificate authority.

Enable Transparent Data Encryption for Oracle Databases

Oracle databases offer a feature called transfer data encryption for encrypting data before storing it on disk. This feature is available in some versions of Oracle. It uses a two-tier key structure for securing encryption keys. Data is encrypted using the table key and this table key is encrypted by using the master key. CloudHSM can be used to store this master encryption key.

Amazon Macie

Amazon Macie is the newest security service powered by Artificial Intelligence launched by AWS that uses machine learning to identify, categorize, and secure your sensitive data that is stored in S3 buckets. It continuously monitors your data and sends alerts when it detects an anomaly in the usage or access patterns. It uses templated Lambda functions for either sending alerts, revoking unauthorized access, or resetting password policies upon detecting suspicious behavior.

As of now, Amazon Macie supports S3 and CloudTrail with the support for more services such as EC2, DynamoDB, RDS, Glue is planned in the near future. Let us look at two important features of Amazon Macie.

Data Discovery and Classification

Amazon Macie allows you to discover and classify sensitive data along with analyzing usage patterns and user behavior. It continuously monitors newly added data to your existing data storage.

It uses artificial intelligence to understand and analyze usage patterns of existing data in the AWS environment. It understands data by using the **Natural Language Processing (NLP)** method.

It will classify sensitive data and prioritize it according to your unique organizational data access patterns. You can use it to create your own alerts and policy definitions for securing your data.

Data Security

Amazon Macie allows you to be proactively compliant with security and achieve preventive security. It enables you to discover, classify, and secure multiple data types such as personally identifiable information, protected health information, compliance documents, audit reports, encryption keys, API keys, and so on.

You can audit instantly by verifying compliance with logs that are automated. All the changes to ACL and security policies can be identified easily. You can configure actionable alerts to detect changes in user behavior.

You can also configure notifications when your protected data leaves the secured zone. You can detect events when an unusual amount of sensitive data is shared either internally or externally.

Summary

Data security is one of the major requirements for most of the AWS users. The AWS platform provides multiple options to secure data in their data storage services for data at rest and data in transit. We learned about securing data for most popular storage services such as AWS S3, AWS RDS, and so on.

We learned the fundamentals of data encryption and how AWS KMS provides a fully managed solution for creating encryption keys, managing, controlling, and auditing usage of these encryption keys.

We also learned about AWS CloudHSM, a dedicated hardware appliance to store your encryption keys for corporate or regulatory compliance. We went through various features of CloudHSM and the most popular use cases for this service.

Lastly, we went through Amazon Macie, a newly launched data security service that uses machine learning for protecting your critical data by automatically detecting and classifying it.

The AWS EC2 service provides compute or servers in AWS for purposes such as web servers, database servers, application servers, monitoring servers, and so on. The EC2 is offered as IaaS in AWS. In the next lesson, *Securing Servers in AWS*, we will look at options to protect your infrastructure in an AWS environment from various internal and external threats. There are host of AWS services dedicated to secure your servers; we will dive deep into these services.

Assessments

1. Which among the following is used for creating and controlling keys used for data encryption in AWS?

    1. IAM
    2. HSM
    3. KMS
    4. S3

2. Asymmetric encryption is also known as _____.

    1. Private key encryption
    2. Public key encryption
    3. Secret key encryption
    4. Data key encryption

3. For encrypting data in AWS, which among the following is used to convert plaintext data into cipher text using the encryption algorithm?

    1. Cipher text private key

    2. Cipher text public key

    3. Plaintext private key

    4. Plaintext data key

4. For decrypting data in AWS, cipher text uses the _____ for converting cipher text into plaintext by applying the decryption algorithm.

    1. Plaintext public key

    2. Plaintext data key

    3. Plaintext private key

    4. Plaintext secret key

5. State whether the following statement is True or False: AWS uses envelope encryption to encrypt data directly.

3
Securing Servers in AWS

The **Amazon Elastic Compute Cloud (EC2)** web service provides secure, elastic, scalable computing capacity in the form of virtual computing environments known as instances in the AWS cloud. EC2 is the backbone of AWS, in a way, so that it drives a majority of the revenue for AWS. This service enables users to run their web applications on a cloud by renting servers. EC2 is part of the **Infrastructure as a Service (IaaS)** offering from AWS, and it provides complete control over the instance provided to the user.

These servers or instances are used for a variety of use cases, such as running web applications, installing various software, running databases, and file storage. EC2 has various benefits as follows that make it quite popular:

- Secured service offering multiple options for securing servers
- Elastic web scale computing; no need to guess the computing capacity
- Complete control over your EC2 instance
- Multiple instance types for various scenarios
- Integration with other AWS services
- Reliable service, offering 99.95% availability for each region
- Inexpensive, offering pay-what-you-use and pay-as-you-use models

Since most of the workloads in AWS run or use EC2 one way or another, it is critical to secure your servers. AWS provides multiple options to secure your servers from numerous threats and gives you the ability to test these security measures as well. Securing servers is essentially securing your infrastructure in AWS. It involves accessing your EC2 instances, monitoring activities on your EC2 instances, and protecting them from external threats such as hacking, **Distributed Denial of Service (DDoS)** attacks, and so on.

With the Amazon EC2 service, users can launch virtual machines with various configurations in the AWS cloud. AWS users have full control over these elastic and scalable virtual machines, also known as EC2 instances.

In this lesson, you are going to learn about best practices and ways to secure EC2 instances in the cloud. AWS provides security for EC2 instances at multiple levels, such as in the operating system of the physical host, in the operating system of the virtual machine, and through multiple firewalls to ensure all API calls are signed. Each of these security measures is built on the capabilities of other security measures.

Our goal is to secure data stored and transferred from an AWS EC2 instance so that it reaches its destination without being intercepted by malicious systems while also maintaining the flexibility of the AWS EC2 instance, along with other AWS services. Our servers in AWS should always be protected from ever-evolving threats and vulnerabilities.

We will dive deep into the following areas of EC2 security:

- IAM roles for EC2
- Managing OS-level access to Amazon EC2 instances
- Protecting the system from malware
- Securing your infrastructure
- Intrusion detection and prevention systems
- Elastic load balancing security
- Building threat protection layers
- Test security

In *Lesson 1, AWS Virtual Private Cloud*, we looked at ways to secure your network in the AWS cloud. We looked at **network access control list (NACL)** and security groups as two firewalls provided by AWS for subnets and EC2 instances, respectively. In this lesson, we are going to dig deeper into security groups. We will also look at other ways to protect your infrastructure in the cloud.

We will look into AWS Inspector, an agent-based and API-driven service that automatically assesses security and vulnerabilities for applications deployed on EC2 instances. We will cover the following topics for AWS Inspector service:

- Features and benefits
- Components

Next, you will learn about AWS Shield, a managed DDoS protection service that will help you minimize downtime and latency for your applications running on EC2 instances and for your AWS resources, such as EC2 instances, **Elastic Load Balancer (ELB)**, Route 53, and so on. We will cover the following topics for the AWS Shield service:

- Benefits
- Key features

EC2 Security Best Practices

There are general best practices for securing EC2 instances that are applicable irrespective of operating system or whether instances are running on virtual machines or on on-premise data centers. Let's look at these general best practices:

- **Least access**: Unless required, ensure that your EC2 instance has restricted access to the instance, as well as restricted access to the network. Provide access only to trusted entities, including software and operating system components that are required to be installed on these instances.

- **Least privilege**: Always follow the principle of least privilege required by your instances, as well as users, to perform their functions. Use role-based access for your instances and create roles with limited permissions. Control and monitor user access for your instances.

- **Configuration management**: Use AWS configuration management services to have a baseline for your instance configuration and treat each EC2 instance as a configuration item. This base configuration should include the updated version of your anti-virus software, security patches, and so on. Keep assessing the configuration of your instance against baseline configuration periodically. Make sure you are generating, storing, and processing logs and audit data.

- **Change management**: Ensure that automated change management processes are in place in order to detect changes in the server configuration. Create rules using AWS services to roll back any changes that are not in line with accepted server configuration or changes that are not authorized.

- **Audit logs**: Ensure that all changes to the server are logged and audited. Use AWS logging and auditing features, such as AWS CloudTrail and VPC flow logs, for logging all API requests and AWS VPC network traffic, respectively.

- **Network access**: AWS provides three options to secure network access for your EC2 instances, security groups, network access control lists, and route tables. An **Elastic Network Interface (ENI)** connected to your instance provides network connectivity to an AWS VPC.

    ° Configure security group rules to allow minimum traffic for your instance. For example, if your EC2 instance is a web server, allow only HTTP and HTTPS traffic.

    ° Use network access control lists as a second layer of defense, as these are stateless and needs more maintenance. Use them to deny traffic from unwanted sources.

    ° Configure route tables for the subnet in your VPC to ensure that instance-specific conditions are met by distinct route tables. For example, create a route table for internet access and associate it with all subnets that require access to the internet.

- **AWS API access from EC2 instances**: Quite often, applications running on EC2 instances would need to access multiple AWS services programmatically by making API calls. AWS recommends that you create roles for these applications, as roles are managed by AWS and credentials are rotated multiple times in a day. Moreover, with roles, there is no need to store credentials locally on an EC2 instance.

- **Data encryption**: Any data that is either stored on or transmitted through an EC2 instance should be encrypted. Use **Elastic Block Storage (EBS)** volumes to encrypt your data at rest through the AWS **Key Management Service (KMS)**. To secure data in transit through encryption, use **Transport Layer Security (TLS)** or IPsec encryption protocols. Ensure that all connections to your EC2 instances are encrypted by configuring outbound rules for security groups.

EC2 Security

An EC2 instance comprises many components: the most prominent ones are the **Amazon Machine Image (AMI)**, the preconfigured software template for your server containing the operating system and software; the hardware including the processor, memory, storage, and networking components based on your requirements; persistent or ephemeral storage volumes for storing your data; the IP addresses, VPCs and virtual and physical location for your instance, such as its subnet, availability zone, and regions, respectively.

When an instance is launched, it is secured by creating a key pair and configuring the security group, a virtual firewall for your instance. In order to access your instance, you will be required to authenticate using this key pair, as depicted in the following figure:

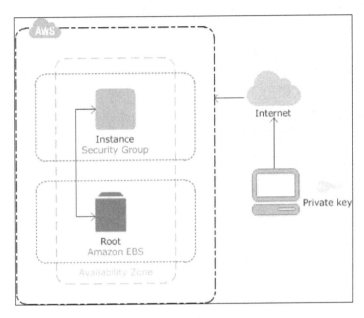

Figure 1: AWS EC2 security

EC2 instances interact with various AWS services and cater to multiple scenarios and use cases across industries, and this universal usability opens up a host of security vulnerabilities for an EC2 instance. AWS provides options for addressing all such vulnerabilities. Let's look at all of these options in detail.

IAM Roles for EC2 Instances

If an application is running on an EC2 instance, it must pass credentials along with its API request. These credentials can be stored in the EC2 instance and managed by developers. Developers have to ensure that these credentials are securely passed to every EC2 instance and are rotated for every instance as well. This is a lot of overhead, which leaves room for errors and security breaches at multiple points.

Alternatively, you can use IAM roles for this purpose. IAM roles provide temporary credentials for accessing AWS resources. IAM roles do not store credentials on instances, and credentials are managed by AWS, so they are automatically rotated multiple times in a day. When an EC2 instance is launched, it is assigned an IAM role. This role will have required permissions to access the desired AWS resource. You can also attach an IAM role to an instance while it is running.

In the following figure, an IAM role to access an S3 bucket is created for an EC2 instance. The developer launches an instance with this role. The application running on this instance uses temporary credentials to access content in the S3 bucket.

In this scenario, the developer is not using long-term credentials that are stored in EC2 instances, thus making this transaction more secure.

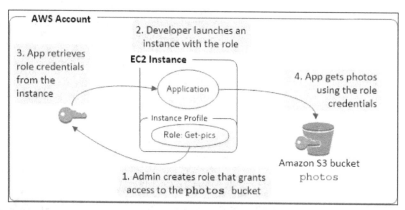

Figure 2: IAM role for EC2 instance

Managing OS-Level Access to Amazon EC2 Instances

Accessing the operating system of an EC2 instance requires different credentials than applications running on an EC2 instance. AWS lets you use your own credentials for the operating system; however, AWS helps you to bootstrap for initial access to the operating system. You can access the operating system of your instance using secure remote system access protocols such as Windows **Remote Desktop Protocol (RDP)** or **Secure Shell (SSH)**.

You can set up the following methods for authenticating operating system access:

- X.509 certificate authentication
- Local operating system accounts
- Microsoft active directory

AWS provides key pairs for enabling authentication to the EC2 instance. These keys can be generated by AWS or by you; AWS stores the public key, and you store the private key. You can have multiple key pairs for authenticating access to multiple instances. For enhanced security, you can also use LDAP or active directory authentication as alternative methods for authentication, instead of the AWS key pair authentication mechanism.

Protecting Your Instance from Malware

An instance in the AWS cloud should be protected from malware (that is, viruses, trojans, spams, and so on), just like any server would be protected in your data center. Having an instance infected with a malware can have far-reaching implications on your entire infrastructure on the cloud.

When a user runs code on an EC2 instance, this executable code assumes the privileges of this user and it can carry out any action that can be carried out by this user based on the user privileges. So, as a rule of thumb, always run code that is trusted and verified with proper code review procedures on your EC2 instances.

If you are using an AMI to launch an EC2 instance, you must ensure this AMI is safe and trusted. Similarly, always install and run trusted software; download this software from trusted and established entities. You could create software depots for all your trusted software and prevent users from downloading software from random sources on the internet.

Ensure all your public facing instances and applications are patched with the latest security configurations and that these patches are revisited regularly and frequently. An infected instance can be used to send spam, a large number of unsolicited emails. This scenario can be prevented by avoiding SMTP open relay (insecure relay or third-party relay), which is usually used to spread spam.

Always keep your antivirus software, along with your anti-spam software updated from reputed and trusted sources on your EC2 instance.

In the event of your instance getting infected, use your antivirus software to remove the virus. Back up all your data and reinstall all the software, including applications, platforms, and so on, from a trusted source, and restore data from your backup. This approach is recommended and widely used in the event of an infected EC2 instance.

Secure Your Infrastructure

AWS lets you create your own virtual private network in the AWS cloud, as you learned in *Lesson 1, AWS Virtual Private Cloud*. VPC enables you to secure your infrastructure on the cloud using multiple options, such as security groups, network access control lists, route tables, and so on. Along with securing infrastructure, VPC also allows you to establish a secure connection with your data center outside of the AWS cloud or with your infrastructure in other AWS accounts. These connections could be through AWS direct connect or through the internet.

Security groups should be used to control traffic allowed for an instance or group of instances performing similar functions, such as web servers or database servers. A security group is a virtual, instance-level firewall. It is assigned to an instance when an instance is launched. You could assign more than one security group to an instance. Rules of security groups can be changed anytime, and they are applied immediately to all instances attached to that security group.

AWS recommends that you use security groups as the first line of defense for an EC2 instance. Security groups are stateful, so responses for an allowed inbound rule will always be allowed irrespective of the outbound rule, and if an instance sends a request, the response for that request will be allowed irrespective of inbound rule configuration.

The following figure shows a security group `SL-Web-SG` configured for all web servers inside a VPC. There are three rules configured; HTTP and HTTPS traffic are allowed from the internet, and SSH for accessing this instance is allowed only from a public IP, that is, `118.185.136.34`.

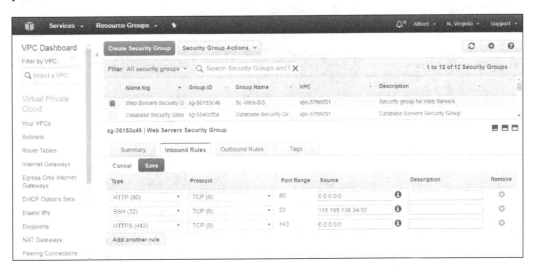

Figure 3: AWS security groups

Each AWS account has a default security group for the default VPC in every region. If you do not specify a security group for your instance, this default security group automatically gets associated with your EC2 instance. This default security group allows all inbound traffic from instances where the source is this default security group. Alongside, it allows all outbound traffic from your EC2 instance. You can modify rules for this default security group, but you cannot delete it.

Security groups are versatile in nature; they allow multiple options for sources for inbound access and destinations for outbound access. Apart from the IP address or range of IP addresses, you can also enter another security group as an object reference for source or destination in order to allow traffic for instances in your security group. However, this process will not add any rules to the current security group from the source security group.

The following figure depicts this example, where we have a security group for database servers; this security group allows traffic only from a web servers security group. In this configuration, the web servers security group is an object reference for the source field, so all the instances that are associated with the database security group will always allow traffic from all instances associated with the web servers security group.

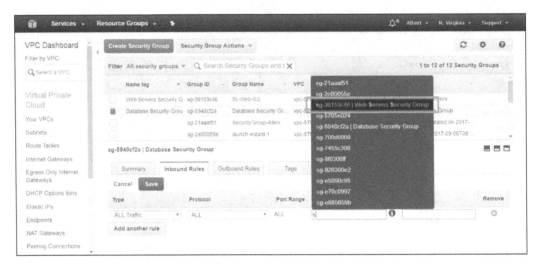

Figure 4: AWS security groups object reference

Intrusion Detection and Prevention Systems

An **Intrusion Detection System** (**IDS**) is a detective and monitoring control that continuously scans your network, servers, platform, and systems for any security breach or violation of security policy, such as a configuration change or malicious activity. If it detects an anomaly, it will report it to the security team.

An **Intrusion Prevention System** (**IPS**), on the other hand, is a preventive control. These controls are placed inside your network, behind organizations' firewalls, and act as a firewall for all known issues and threats related to incoming traffic. All traffic needs to pass IPS in order to reach their destination. If an IPS finds traffic to contain malicious content, it will block that traffic.

The AWS marketplace offers various IDS and IPS products to secure your network and systems. These products help you detect vulnerabilities in your EC2 instances by deploying host-based IDS and by employing behavioral monitoring techniques.

These products also help you secure your AWS EC2 instances from attacks by deploying next-generation firewalls in your network, which have features such as full stack visibility for all layers in your infrastructure.

Elastic Load Balancing Security

An **Elastic Load Balancer** (**ELB**) is a managed AWS service that automatically distributes incoming traffic to targets behind a load balancer across all availability zones in a region. These targets could be EC2 instances, containers, and IP addresses.

An ELB takes care of all encryption and decryption centrally, so there is no additional workload on EC2 instances. An ELB can be associated with AWS VPC and has its own security groups. These security groups can be configured in a similar way to EC2 security groups with inbound and outbound rules.

Alongside, ELB also supports end-to-end traffic encryption through the **Transport Layer Security** (**TLS**) protocol for networks using HTTPS connections. In this scenario, you don't need to use an individual instance for terminating client connections while using TLS; instead, you can use ELB to perform the same function. You can create an HTTPS listener for your ELB that will encrypt traffic between your load balancer and clients initiating HTTPS sessions. It will also encrypt traffic between EC2 instances and load balancers serving traffic to these EC2 instances.

Building Threat Protection Layers

Quite often, organizations will have multiple features for securing their infrastructure, network, data, and so on. The AWS cloud gives you various such features in the form of VPC, security groups as virtual firewall for your EC2 instances, NACL as secondary firewalls for your subnets, and host-based firewalls and IDS, along with **Intrusion Prevention System** (**IPS**), for creating your own threat protection layer as part of your security framework.

This threat protection layer will prevent any unwanted traffic from reaching its desired destination, such as an application server or a database server. For example, in the following figure, a corporate user is accessing an application from the corporate data center. This user is connecting to AWS VPC using a secure connection, which could be a VPN connection or a direct connect connection and does not require interception by a threat protection layer.

However, requests made by all users accessing this application through the internet are required to go through a threat protection layer before they reach the presentation layer.

This approach is known as layered network defense on the cloud. This approach is suitable for organizations that need more than what AWS offers out of the box for protecting networking infrastructure. AWS VPC provides you with various features to support the building of your threat protection layer; these features include the following:

- Support for multiple layers of load balancers
- Support for multiple IP addresses
- Support for multiple **Elastic Network Interfaces (ENI)**

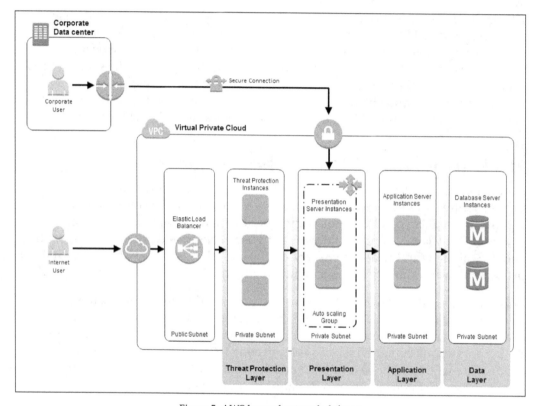

Figure 5: AWS layered network defence

Testing Security

It is imperative for any **Infrastructure Security Management System (ISMS)** to continuously test their security measures and validate them against ever-evolving threats and vulnerabilities. Testing these security measures and controls involves testing the infrastructure and network provided by AWS. AWS recommends that you take the following approaches to test the security of your environment:

- **External vulnerability assessment**: Engage a third party that has no knowledge of your infrastructure and controls deployed. Let this third party test all your controls and systems independently. Use the findings of this engagement to strengthen your security framework.

- **External penetration tests**: Utilize the services of a third party that has no knowledge of your infrastructure and controls deployed to break into your network and servers in a controlled manner. Use these findings to strengthen your security controls deployed for intrusion prevention.

- **Internal gray or white-box review of applications and platforms**: Use an internal resource, a tester, who has knowledge of your security controls to try to break into the security of applications and platforms and expose or discover vulnerabilities.

- **Penetration testing process**: AWS allows you to conduct penetration testing for your own instances; however, you have to request permission from AWS before you conduct any penetration testing. You would have to log in using root credentials for the instance that you want to test and fill an AWS Vulnerability/Penetration Testing Request Form. If you want a third party to conduct these tests, you can fill the details about it in this form as well.

As of now, the AWS penetration testing policy allows testing of the following AWS services:

- Amazon Elastic Compute Cloud
- Amazon Relational Database Service
- Amazon Aurora
- Amazon CloudFront
- Amazon API Gateway
- AWS Lambda
- AWS Lightsail
- DNS Zone Walking

Amazon Inspector

Amazon Inspector is an automated, agent-based security and vulnerability assessment service for your AWS resources. As of now, it supports only EC2 instances. It essentially complements devops culture in an organization, and it integrates with continuous integration and continuous deployment tools.

To begin with, you install an agent in your EC2 instance, prepare an assessment template, and run a security assessment for this EC2 instance.

Amazon Inspector will collect data related to running processes, the network, the filesystem and lot of data related to configuration, the traffic flow between AWS services and network, the secure channels, and so on.

Once this data is collected, it is validated against a set of predefined rules known as the rules package, that you choose in your assessment template, and you are provided with detailed findings and issues related to security, categorized by severity.

The following figure shows the Amazon Inspector splash screen with three steps for getting started with Amazon Inspector:

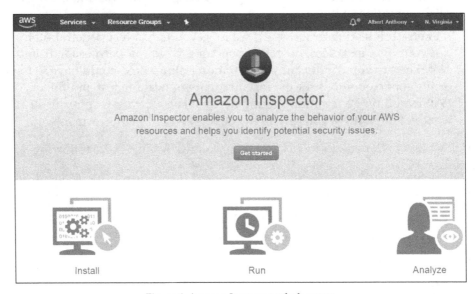

Figure 6: Amazon Inspector splash screen

Amazon Inspector Features and Benefits

Amazon Inspector goes hand in hand with the continuous integration and continuous deployment activities that are essential part of the DevOps life cycle. It helps you integrate security with your DevOps by making security assessment part of your deployment cycle. Amazon Inspector has several important features that make it one of the most preferred security assessment services for any infrastructure in AWS. Let's look at these features:

- **Enforce security standards and compliance**: You can select a security best practices rules package to enforce the most common security standards for your infrastructure. Ensure that assessments are run before any deployment to proactively detect and address security issues before they reach the production environment. You can ensure that security compliance standards are met at every stage of your development life cycle. Moreover, Amazon Inspector provides findings based on real activity and the actual configuration of your AWS resources, so you can rest assured about the compliance of your environment.

- **Increasing development agility**: Amazon Inspector is fully automatable through API. Once you integrate it with your development and deployment process, your security issues and your vulnerabilities are detected and resolved early, resulting in saving a huge amount of resources. These resources can be used to develop new features for your application and release it to your end users, thus increasing the velocity of your development.

- **Leverage AWS Security expertise**: Amazon Inspector is a managed service, so when you select a rules package for assessment, you get assessed for the most updated security issues and vulnerabilities for your EC2 instance. Moreover, these rules packages are constantly updated with ever evolving threats, vulnerabilities, and best practices by the AWS Security organization.

- **Integrated with AWS services and AWS partners**: Amazon Inspector integrates with AWS partners, providing security tools through its public-facing APIs. AWS partners use Amazon Inspector's findings to create email alerts, security status dashboards, pager platforms, and so on. Amazon Inspector works with a **network address translation (NAT)** instance, as well as proxy environments. It also integrates with the AWS **Simple Notification Service (SMS)** for notifications and AWS CloudTrail for recording all API activity.

The following figure shows the Amazon Inspector integration with AWS CloudTrail. All activities related to Amazon Inspector are captured by AWS CloudTrail events.

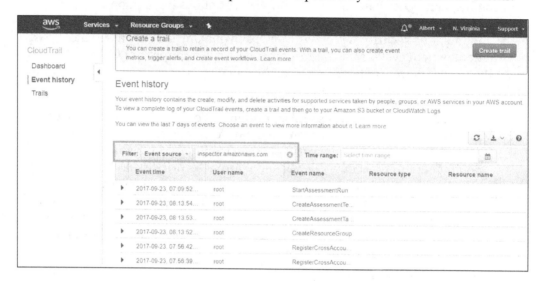

Figure 7: Amazon Inspector CloudTrail events

Amazon Inspector publishes real-time metrics data to AWS CloudWatch so you can analyze metrics for your target (EC2 instance) as well as for your assessment template in AWS CloudWatch. By default, Amazon Inspector sends data to AWS CloudWatch in interval of five minutes. It could be changed to a one minute interval as well.

There are three categories of metrics available in AWS CloudWatch for Amazon Inspector, as follows:

- Assessment target
- Assessment template
- Aggregate

The following figure shows metrics available for assessment targets in AWS CloudWatch:

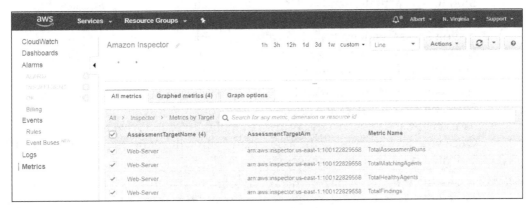

Figure 8: Amazon Inspector CloudWatch metrics

Amazon Inspector Components

Amazon Inspector is accessible the through AWS Management Console, the AWS **Software Development Kit (SDK)**, AWS Command Line Tools, and Amazon Inspector APIs, through HTTPS. Let's look at the major components of this service, as shown in the following figure:

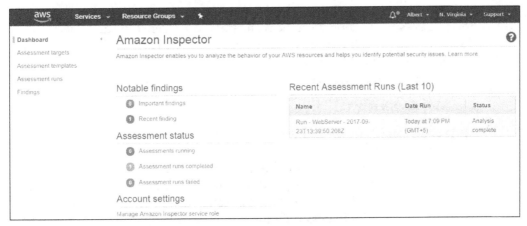

Figure 9: Amazon Inspector dashboard

- **AWS agent**: This is a software agent developed by AWS that must be installed in your assessment target, that is, your EC2 instance. This agent monitors all activities and collects data for your EC2 instance, such as the installation, configuration, and filesystem, as per the rules package selected by you for assessment. It periodically sends this data to the Amazon Inspector service. AWS Agent simply collects data; it does not change anything in the EC2 instance it is running.

- **Assessment run**: You will periodically run assessments on your EC2 instance based on the rules package selected. Once your AWS agent performs assessment, it discovers any security vulnerabilities in your EC2 instance. Once you have completed the assessment, you will get findings, with a list of potential issues and their severity.

- **Assessment target**: Amazon Inspect or requires you to select an assessment target; this is your EC2 instance or a group of EC2 instances that will be assessed for any potential security issues. These instances should be tagged with key value pairs. You can create up to 50 assessment targets per AWS account.

- **Finding**: A finding is a potential security issue reported by Amazon Inspector service after running an assessment for your target EC2 instance. These findings are displayed in the Amazon Inspector web console or can be accessed through API. These findings contain details about the issue, along with its severity and recommendations to fix it.

- **Assessment report**: This is a document that details what all was tested for an assessment, along with the results of those tests. You can generate assessment reports for all assessments once they are completed successfully. There are two types of assessment reports:
    - The findings report
    - The full report

- **Rules package**: Amazon Inspector has a repository of hundreds of rules, divided under four rules packages. These rules packages are the knowledge base of the most common security and vulnerability definitions. Your assessment target is checked against the rules of a rules package. These rules packages are constantly updated by the Amazon security team, as and when new threats, security issues, and vulnerabilities are identified or discovered. These four rules packages are shown in the following figure:

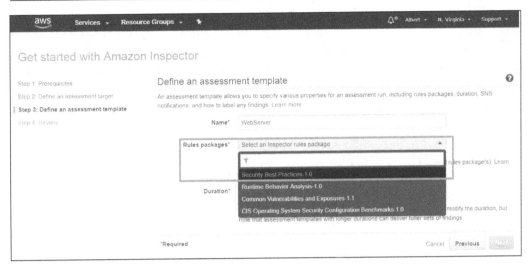

Figure 10: Amazon Inspector rules packages

- **Rules**: Amazon Inspector has predefined rules in the rules packages; as of now, custom rules cannot be defined for a rules package. A rule is a check performed by an Amazon Inspector agent on an assessment target during an assessment. If a rule finds a security issue, it will add this issue to findings. Every rule has a security level assigned to it. There are four security levels for a rule, as follows:
  - ○ High
  - ○ Medium
  - ○ Low
  - ○ Informational

  A high, medium, or low security level indicates an issue that might cause an interruption in the ways in which your services are required to run. An informational security level describes the security configuration for your instance.

- **Assessment template**: This is your configuration for running an assessment. You will choose your targets, along with one of the four predefined rules packages that you want to run; you will also choose a duration, from 15 minutes to 24 hours, and other information, as shown in the following figure:

Figure 11: Amazon Inspector assessment template

AWS Shield

AWS Shield is a managed **Distributed Denial of Service (DDoS)** protection service. It detects and automatically mitigates attacks that could potentially result in downtime for your application and might also increase latency for your applications running on EC2 instances.

A DDoS attack results in increased traffic for your EC2 instances, Elastic Load Balancer, Route 53, or CloudFront. As a result, these services would need to scale up resources to cope with the increased traffic. A DDoS attack usually happens when multiple systems are compromised or infected with a Trojan flooding a target system with an intention to deny a service to intended users by generating traffic and shutting down a resource so it cannot serve more requests.

AWS Shield has two tiers: **Standard** and **Advanced**. All protection under the AWS Shield Standard option is available to all AWS customers by default, without any additional charge. The AWS Shield Advanced option is available to customers with business and enterprise support at an additional charge. The advanced option provides protection against more sophisticated attacks on your AWS resources, such as an EC2 instance, ELB, and so on. The following figure shows AWS Shield tiers:

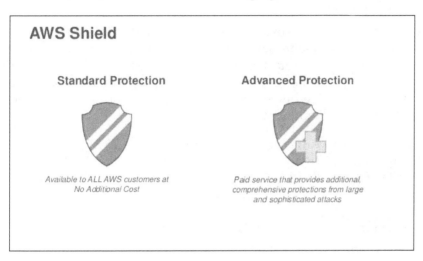

Figure 12: AWS shield tiers

AWS Shield Benefits

AWS Shield is covered under the AWS suite of services that are eligible for **Health Insurance Portability and Accounting Act (HIPAA)** compliance. It can be used to protect websites hosted outside of AWS, as it is integrated with AWS CloudFront. Let's look at other benefits of AWS Shield:

- **Seamless integration and deployment**: AWS Shield Standard automatically secures your AWS resources with the most common and regular DDoS attacks in network and transport layers. If you require enhanced security for more sophisticated attacks, you can opt for the AWS Shield Advanced option for your AWS resources, such as EC2 Instances, Route 53 AWS CloudFront, and so on, by enabling the AWS Shield Advanced option from the AWS Management Console or through APIs.

- **Customizable protection**: You can script your own customized rules to address sophisticated attacks on your AWS resources using the AWS Shield Advanced tier. You can deploy these rules immediately to avoid any imminent threat, such as by blocking bad traffic or for automating response to security incidents. You could also take the help of the AWS **DDoS Response Team (DRT)** to write the rules for you. This team is available for your support 24/7.

- **Cost efficient**: AWS provides free protection against network layer attacks for all its customers through AWS Shield Standard. With AWS Shield Advanced, you get protection against DDoS Cost Escalation, which prevents your cost going up in case of DDoS attacks. However, if you are billed for any of your AWS resource usage due to a DDoS attack, you can request credits from AWS through the AWS support channel.

The AWS Shield Advanced billing plan starts at USD $3000 per month. Charges for data transfer are calculated separately for all AWS resources selected for the AWS Shield advanced protection.

AWS Shield Features

Let's look at AWS Shield features for Standard and Advanced tiers:

- **AWS Shield Standard**:
    - ° **Quick detection**: AWS Shield Standard automatically inspects all traffic for your AWS resources through its continuous network flow monitoring feature. It detects any malicious traffic through a combination of advanced algorithms, specific analysis, traffic signatures, and so on in real time, to prevent you from the most common and frequent attacks.
    - ° **Inline attack mitigation**: AWS Shield Standard gives you protection against Layer 3 and Layer 4 attacks that occur at the infrastructure layer through its automated mitigation processes. These processes do not have any impact on performance, such as the latency of your AWS resources, as they are applied inline for your applications. Inline mitigation helps you avoid the downtime for your AWS resources and your applications running on these AWS resources.

- **AWS Shield Advanced**:
  - **Enhanced detection**: This feature helps with detecting DDoS attacks on the application layer, such as HTTP floods, as well as with monitoring and verifying network traffic flow.
  - **Advanced attack mitigation**: For protection against large DDoS attacks, AWS Shield advanced provides protection automatically by applying advanced routing processes. You also have access to the AWS **DDoS Response Team (DRT)**, which can help you mitigate more sophisticated and advanced DDoS attacks manually. DRT can work with you to diagnose and manually mitigate attacks on your behalf.

You can also enable AWS Shield advanced on your multiple AWS accounts as long as all of these accounts are under one single billing account and are owned by you, and all AWS resources in these accounts are owned by you.

With AWS Shield advanced, you get a history of all incidents in your AWS account for the past 13 months. As it is integrated with AWS CloudWatch, you get a notification through AWS CloudWatch metrics as soon as an attack happens. This notification will be sent in a matter of a few minutes.

Summary

In this lesson, you learned about various features and services available in AWS to secure your servers, most notably, EC2 instances. We went through best practices to follow for EC2 security.

Alongside, we dove deep into various measures to follow for all use cases for securing your EC2 instances. These measures range from using IAM roles for all applications running on EC2 instances to managing operating system access to building threat protection layers in your multi-layered architectures and testing security for your EC2 instances with prior permission from AWS support.

You learned about Amazon Inspector, an automated security assessment managed service that integrates security assessment, identification, and remediation with development. This results in faster deployment and better agility for your development process. You learned about the various components of Amazon Inspector, such as agents, assessment template, findings, and so on, to help use this service for EC2 instances.

Lastly, we went through AWS Shield, a managed DDoS protection service, along with its features and benefits. You learned about the AWS Shield tiers, Standard and Advanced, and how they can protect AWS resources from the most common, as well as the most advanced and sophisticated, attacks. In this section, you learned about AWS DRT, a team available 24/7 to help us mitigate attacks and respond to incidents that can also write code for us if required.

In the next lesson, *Securing Applications in AWS*, you are going to learn about various AWS services provided to AWS customers for securing applications running on AWS. These could be a monolithic application, a web or a mobile application, a serverless application, or a microservices-based application. These applications could run entirely on AWS, or they could run in a hybrid mode, that is, partially in AWS and partially outside of AWS.

These applications might run on various AWS resources and interact with various AWS resources, such as applications running on EC2 instances that store data on AWS S3. This scenario opens up the possibility of attacks from various channels. AWS has a whole suite of services and features to thwart all such attacks, including application-level firewalls, managed services for user authentication, managed services for securing APIs, and so on.

Assessments

1. If an application is running on an EC2 instance, it must pass credentials along with its _____.

    1. API response

    2. API request

    3. IP address

    4. VPC credentials

2. When an EC2 instance is launched, it is assigned to which role?

    1. HSM

    2. KMS

    3. S3

    4. IAM

3. Which among the following enables you to secure your infrastructure on the cloud using multiple options?

    1. Subnet

    2. NAT

    3. VPC

    4. ENI

4. Which among the following is a detective and monitoring control system that continuously scans your network, servers, platform, and systems?

    1. IDS

    2. IPS

    3. ELB

    4. ISMS

5. State whether the following is True or False: AWS Shield is a managed Distributed Denial of Service (DDoS) protection service.

4
Securing Applications in AWS

AWS gives you multiple services, features, and tools to build scalable, de-coupled, and secure cloud applications. AWS supports web application development in programming languages such as Python, JAVA, .NET, PHP, Ruby, and mobile application development as well as Android and iOS platforms by providing **Software Development Kits (SDKs)**. Alongside this, it provides the following tools for developing applications in the AWS cloud environment:

- **Integrated development environments (IDEs)** such as Visual Studio and Eclipse

- Command-line tools such as AWS CLI, AWS tools for PowerShell, and so on

- Services for running these applications, such as Elastic Compute Cloud, AWS Elastic Beanstalk, and Amazon EC2 Container Service

- Tools and services for developing serverless applications such as AWS **Serverless Application Model (SAM)** and AWS Lambda respectively

- Managed services such as AWS CodeCommit for source control and AWS CodeDeploy for automation of code deployment process

When you develop and deploy web and mobile applications in the cloud using the above-mentioned services, tools, and features, you need to secure it from SQL injections, unwanted traffic, intrusions, **Distributed Denial of Service (DDoS)** attacks, and other similar threats. Furthermore, you need to ensure that all requests sent to AWS through your applications are secure and recognized by AWS as authorized requests. Your applications that are deployed on EC2 instances should be able to communicate securely with other AWS services such as the **Simple Storage Service (S3)** or **Relational Database Service (RDS)**. Securing applications in AWS is as critical as securing your data and infrastructure in AWS.

In this lesson, we will learn about securing web and mobile applications in AWS cloud. We will begin with **Web Application Firewall (WAF)**, an AWS service that secures your web applications from common threats by creating access control lists to filter threats. We will learn the following about AWS WAF:

* Benefits of AWS WAF
* Working with AWS WAF
* Security automation with AWS WAF

Moving on we will walk you through securing API requests by learning to sign these requests while communicating with AWS services and resources.

Furthermore, we will learn about a couple of AWS services, as follows, that are extremely useful in securing our applications in the cloud.

* **Amazon Cognito**: A managed AWS service for authenticating user data for your mobile applications.

* **Amazon API Gateway**: A managed AWS service for securing, creating, and managing APIs.

AWS Web Application Firewall

AWS WAF is a web application firewall that helps you define various rules in the form of conditions and access control lists to secure your web applications from common security threats, such as cross-site scripting, DDoS attacks, SQL injections, and so on. These threats may result in application unavailability or an application consuming excessive resources due to an increase in malicious web traffic.

You secure your websites and web applications by monitoring, controlling, and filtering HTTP and HTTPS requests received by the Application Load Balancer and Amazon CloudFront. You can allow or reject these requests based on various filters, such as the IP address sending these requests, header values, URI strings, and so on. These security features do not impact the performance of your web applications.

AWS WAF enables you to perform three behaviors--allowing all requests other than the ones that are specified by the access control lists; blocking all requests other than the ones that have been allowed access by the access control lists; counting all requests that are allowable as per the rules set in access control lists. You can use AWS WAF to secure websites hosted outside of the AWS cloud environment, as Amazon CloudFront supports origins outside of AWS. You can configure the Amazon CloudFront to display a custom error page when a request matches your WAF rule and then block it.

It is integrated with CloudWatch and CloudTrail so you can monitor the WAF metrics in real time, such as the number of blocked requests and near real-time and historical audit logs of WAF API respectively. The following figure shows the AWS WAF workflow:

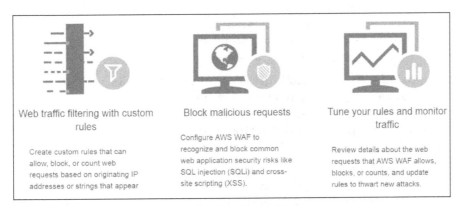

Web traffic filtering with custom rules

Create custom rules that can allow, block, or count web requests based on originating IP addresses or strings that appear

Block malicious requests

Configure AWS WAF to recognize and block common web application security risks like SQL injection (SQLi) and cross-site scripting (XSS).

Tune your rules and monitor traffic

Review details about the web requests that AWS WAF allows, blocks, or counts, and update rules to thwart new attacks.

Figure 1: AWS Web Application Firewall

Benefits of AWS Web Application Firewall

Let us look at the most popular benefits of AWS WAF:

- **Increased protection against web attacks**: You get protection for your web applications through AWS WAF. It will filter the web traffic based on the access control lists and rules that you can configure for most common web exploits, such as blocking specific IP addresses or blocking matching query strings containing malicious web traffic, and so on.

- **Security integrated with how you develop applications**: AWS WAF enables you to configure all of its features through its APIs and through the AWS Management Console. It also imbibes the culture of DevSecOps in your organization as the development team takes ownership of securing applications by using WAF and adding rules at multiple areas and levels throughout the application development cycle. So you have a developer writing code and adding WAF rules, a DevOps engineer that will deploy this code, and a security auditor who will audit all application security in place of web applications.

- **Ease of deployment and maintenance**: AWS WAF is integrated with Amazon CloudFront and the Application Load Balancer. This makes it easy for you to deploy web applications by making them part of your Content Delivery Network (CDN) or by using the Application Load Balancer that is used to front all your web servers. You do not need to install any additional software on any servers or anywhere in your AWS environment. Moreover, you can write rules in one place and deploy them across all your web applications hosted across various resources in your AWS environment.

- **Improved web traffic visibility**: You can set up metrics and dashboards for all your web application requests that are evaluated against your WAF rules in Amazon CloudWatch. You can monitor these metrics in near real-time and gauge the health of your web traffic. You can also use this metrics information to modify the existing WAF rules or create new ones.

- **Cost effective web application development**: AWS WAF prevents you from creating, managing, and deploying your own custom web monitoring and firewall solution. It allows you to save development costs for your custom web application firewall solution. AWS WAF, like other AWS services, allows you to pay only for what you use without any upfront commitment or a minimum fee. It has a flexible pricing model depending on the number of rules deployed and traffic received by your web application in terms of HTTP and HTTPS requests.

Working with AWS Web Application Firewall

When working with AWS WAF, you begin by creating conditions for matching malicious traffic; next, you combine one or more of these conditions as rules and these rules are combined as web access control lists. These web access control lists can be associated with one or multiple resources in your AWS environment such as Application Load Balancers or CloudFront web distributions.

- **Conditions**: You can define one of the following conditions available in AWS WAF when you would either want to allow or block requests based on these conditions:
    - Cross-site scripting
    - Geo match
    - IP addresses
    - Size constraints
    - SQL injection
    - String and regex matching

The following figure shows an example of an IP address condition where multiple suspicious IP addresses are listed. You can list one IP address as well as range of IP addresses in your conditions.

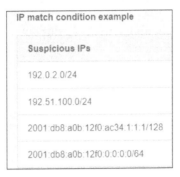

Figure 2: AWS WAF condition

- **Rules**: You combine conditions to create rules for requests that you want to either allow, block, or count. There are two types of rules:
    - **Regular rules**: These rules are created by combining conditions only. For example, a regular rule will contain requests originating from a specific IP address.
    - **Rate-based rules**: These rules are similar to regular rules with the addition of a rate limit. Essentially, these rules count the requests every 5 minutes originating from a source and, this enables you to take an action based on the pre-defined rate limit for a rule.

The following diagram shows a couple of rules in the AWS WAF dashboard:

Figure 3: AWS WAF rules

- **Web ACL**: A set of rules combined together forms a web ACL. You define an action such as allow, block, or count for each rule. Along with these actions, you also define a default action for each rule of your web ACL in scenarios when a request does not meet any of the three conditions for a rule.

The following figure (available in AWS documentation) shows a web ACL containing a rate based rule and regular rules. It also shows how it evaluates the condition for these rules and how it performs actions based on these checks:

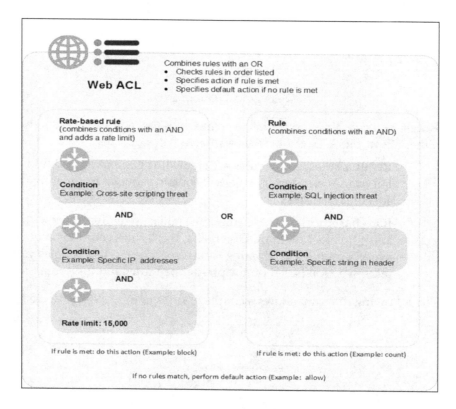

Figure 4: AWS WAF Web ACL

Signing AWS API Requests

API requests sent to AWS should include a digital signature that contains information about the requestor's identity. This identity is verified by AWS for all API requests. This process is known as signing API requests. For all API requests generated through AWS tools, such as AWS SDKs and AWS Command Line Interface, the digital signature is included for you, however, for all API requests that you create manually, you have to include this digital signature yourself.

In other words, you need to sign your HTTP requests when you create them. You need to do this if you are writing a code in a programming language that does not have an AWS SDK. Furthermore, if you need to control what is sent along with an API request, you can choose to sign requests yourself.

A digital signature includes your AWS access keys, that is, your secret access key and access key ID, along with API information. An API request should reach the AWS within 15 minutes of the timestamp stored in this request, otherwise it is rejected by AWS.

There are certain anonymous API requests that do not include digital signatures with identity information, such as anonymous requests to S3 or to API operations requests in the **Security Token Service (STS)**.

Requests are signed to secure your communication with AWS in the following ways:

- Verifying the requestor's identity
- Protecting the data in transit
- Protection against potential replay attacks

AWS recommends using signature version 4 that uses the `HMAC-SHA256` protocol for signing all your requests. It supports signature version 4 and signature version 2.

You sign a request by calculating a hash (digest) for the request. Then you calculate another hash, also known as a signature, by using the previous hash value, information from the request, and your access key. This signature is then added to the request by using either the HTTP Header (authorization) or by adding a query string value to this request.

Amazon Cognito

Amazon Cognito is a managed service that allows you to quickly add users for your mobile and web applications by providing in-built sign-in screens and authentication functionality. It handles security, authorization, and synchronization for your user management process across devices for all your users. You can use Cognito for authenticating your users through external identity providers including social identity providers, such as Facebook, Google, Twitter, LinkedIn, and so on. Cognito can also be used to authenticate identities for any solution that is compatible with SAML 2.0 standard. You can provide temporary security credentials with limited privileges to these authenticated users to securely access your AWS resources. The following figure illustrates three basic functionalities of Amazon Cognito: user management, authentication, and synchronization:

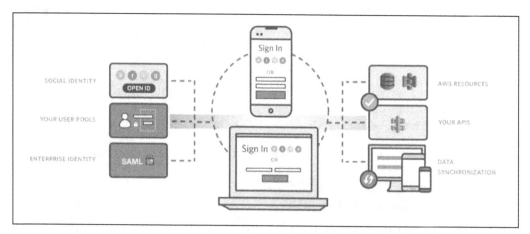

Figure 5: AWS Cognito overview

This service is primarily designed for developers to use in their web and mobile apps. It enables developers to allow users to securely access the app's resources. You begin by creating and configuring a user pool, a user directory for your apps, in Amazon Cognito either through AWS Management Console, AWS CLI, or through AWS SDK. Once you have created user pool, you can download, install, and integrate AWS Mobile SDK with your app, whether on iOS or Android. You also have an option to call APIs directly for Cognito if you do not wish to use SDK, as it exposes all control and data APIs as web services for you to consume them through your own client library.

Amazon Cognito integrates with CloudTrail and CloudWatch so you can monitor Cognito metrics and log API activities in real time and take the required action for any suspicious activity or security threat.

Amazon API Gateway

As a developer, you have to work with APIs on a regular basis. Amazon API Gateway is a fully managed web service that helps to manage, publish, maintain, monitor, and secure APIs for any workload running on EC2 instances, AWS Lambda, or any web application. You can use API Gateway to manage, authenticate, and secure hundreds of thousands of concurrent API calls. Management of APIs includes access control, traffic management, monitoring, and API version management. All the APIs that are built using API Gateway support data over HTTP protocols. You can also run multiple versions of the same REST API by cloning the existing API. Let us look at the following benefits of using Amazon API Gateway:

- **Low cost and efficient**: You pay for the requests that are made to your API, for example, $3.5 per million API calls, along with the cost of data transfer out, in gigabytes. You also have the option to choose cache for your API, and that will incur charges on an hourly basis. Apart from these, there are no upfront commitments or minimum fees. It integrates with Amazon CloudFront, allowing you access to a global network of Edge locations to run your APIs, resulting in a lower latency of API requests and responses for your end users.

- **Flexible security controls**: With API Gateway, you can use AWS Security and administration services, such as IAM and Cognito, for authorizing access to your APIs. Alternatively, you can also use a custom authorizer, such as Lambda functions, for authentication if you already have OAuth tokens or if you are using other authorization processes. It can also verify signed APIs using the same technology that is used by AWS to verify its own calls.

- **Run your APIs without servers**: API Gateway allows you to run your APIs completely without using any servers through its integration with AWS Lambda. You can run your code entirely in AWS Lambda and use API Gateway to create REST APIs for your web and mobile applications. This allows you to focus on writing code instead of managing to compute resources for your application.

- **Monitor APIs**: You can monitor all your APIs after they have been published and are in use through the API Gateway dashboard. It integrates with Amazon CloudWatch to give you near real-time visibility on the performance of your APIs through metrics, such as data latency, error rates, API calls, and so on. Once you enable detailed monitoring for API Gateway, you can use CloudWatch Logs to receive logs for every API method as well. You can also monitor API utilization by third-party developers through the API Gateway dashboard.

Summary

In this lesson, we learned about securing applications that are built on top of AWS resources. We went through WAF in detail to protect web applications in AWS and learned about the benefits and lifecycle of Web Application Firewall. We also walked through the process of automating security with WAF.

Furthermore, we went through the process of signing AWS API requests for securing data in transit along with securing information stored in API itself.

Lastly, we learned about two AWS services that are used by developers to secure their web and mobile applications--Amazon Cognito for user management and Amazon API Gateway for managing and securing APIs.

In the next lesson, *AWS Security Best Practices*, we will learn about AWS security best practices. It will be a culmination of all that we have learned so far in all the previous lessons regarding security in AWS. We will learn about solutions to ensure that best practices are met for all topics such as IAM, VPC, security of data, security of servers, and so on.

Assessments

1. Which among the following supports origins outside of AWS?
    1. WAF
    2. CloudWatch
    3. CloudFront
    4. CloudTrail

2. Web access control lists can be associated with one or multiple resources in your AWS environment such as _____.
    1. WAF
    2. CloudWatch
    3. ELB
    4. Application Load Balancers

3. State whether the following statement is True or False: A set of rules combined together forms a web ACL.

4. API requests sent to AWS should include a _____ that contains information about the requestor's identity.

    1. Digital signature
    2. IP address of the requestor
    3. Private key
    4. Public key

5. Which among the following integrates with CloudTrail and CloudWatch so you can monitor Cognito metrics and log API activities in real time?

    1. AWS Management Console
    2. AWS SDK
    3. AWS CLI
    4. Amazon Cognito

5
AWS Security Best Practices

Security at AWS is job zero. AWS is architected to be one of the most secure cloud environments with a host of built-in security features that allows it to eliminate most of the security overhead that is traditionally associated with IT infrastructure. Security is considered a shared responsibility between AWS and AWS customers where both of them work together to achieve their security objectives. We have looked at various services, tools, features, and third-party solutions provided by AWS to secure your assets on AWS. All customers share the following benefits of AWS security without any additional charges or resources:

- Keeping your data safe
- Meeting compliance requirements
- Saving money with in-built AWS security features
- Scaling quickly without compromising security

An enterprise running business-critical applications on AWS cannot afford to compromise on the security of these applications or the AWS environment where these applications are running. As per Gartner, **by 2020, 95% of all security breaches or incidents in cloud will be due to customer error and not from the cloud provider**.

Security is a core requirement for any **Information Security Management System (ISMS)** to prevent information from unauthorized access; theft, deletion, integrity compromise, and so on. A typical ISMS is not required to use AWS, however, AWS has a set of best practices lined up under the following topics to address widely adopted approaches for ensuring security for ISMS. You can use this approach if you have an ISMS in place.

- What shared security responsibility model is and how it works between AWS and customers
- Categorization and identifying your assets

- How to use privileged accounts and groups to control and manage user access to your data?

- Best practices for securing your data, network, servers, and operating systems

- How to achieve your security objectives using monitoring and alerting?

For more information on best practices on securing your ISMS, refer to the AWS Security Center at `https://aws.amazon.com/security/`. You can also use AWS Security Center for staying updated with the most common security issues and solutions to address these issues.

Security by design: There are the following two broad aspects of security in AWS:

- **Security of AWS environment**: AWS provides many services, tools, and features to secure your entire AWS environment including systems, networks, and resources such as encryption services, logging, configuration rules, identity management, and so on.

- **Security of hosts and applications**: Along with your AWS environment, you also need to secure applications that are running on AWS resources, data stored in the AWS resources, and operating systems on servers in AWS. This responsibility is primarily managed by AWS customers. AWS provides all tools and technologies available on-premises and used by the customer in AWS cloud as well.

Security by design is a four-phase systematic approach to ensure continuous security, compliance, and real-time auditing at scale. It is applicable for the security of AWS environment that allows for automation of security controls and streamlined audit processes. It allows customers to imbibe security and compliance reliably coded into AWS account. The following are four-phases of the Security by design approach:

- Understand your requirements

- Build a secure environment

- Enforce the use of templates

- Perform validation activities

Security in AWS is distributed at multiple layers such as AWS products and services, data security, application security, and so on. It is imperative to follow best practices for securing all such products and services to avoid getting your resources compromised in the AWS cloud.

Security is the number one priority for AWS and it is a shared responsibility between AWS and its customers. Security is imperative for all workloads deployed in the AWS environment. In AWS, storage is cheap, it should be used to store all logs and relevant records. It is recommended to use AWS managed services and in-built reporting services as much as possible for security to offload heavy lifting and enabling automation.

In this lesson, we will go over security best practices in AWS. These best practices are a combination of AWS recommendations, as well as expert advice and most common practices to follow in order to secure your AWS environment.

Our objective is to have a minimum security baseline for our workloads in the AWS environment by following these best practices that are spread across AWS services, products, and features. These security measures allow you to get visibility into the AWS usage and AWS resources and take corrective actions when required. They also allow automation at multiple levels, such as at the infrastructure level or at the application level to enable continuous monitoring and continuous compliance for all workloads deployed in AWS along with all AWS resources used in your AWS account.

We will learn about security best practices for the following topics:

- Shared security responsibility model
- IAM
- VPC
- Data security
- Security of servers
- Application security
- Monitoring, logging, and auditing

We will also look at **Cloud Adoption Framework (CAF)** that helps organizations embarking on their cloud journey with standards, best practices, and so on.

We will learn about the security perspective of CAF along with the following four components:

- Preventive
- Responsive
- Detective
- Directive

Shared Security Responsibility Model

One of the first and most important requirements and security best practice to follow is to know about the AWS shared security responsibility model. Ensure that all stakeholders understand their share of security in AWS.

AWS is responsible for the security of cloud and underlying infrastructure that powers AWS cloud, and customers are responsible for security in the cloud, for anything they put in, and build on top of the AWS global infrastructure.

It is imperative to have clear guidelines about this shared security responsibility model in your organization. Identify resources that fall under your share of responsibilities, define activities that you need to perform, and publish a schedule of these activities to all stakeholders. The following figure shows the AWS shared security responsibility model:

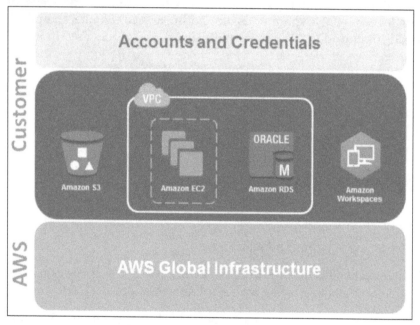

Figure 1: AWS shared security responsibility model

IAM Security Best Practices

IAM provides secure access control in your AWS environment to interact with AWS resources in a controlled manner:

- **Delete your root access keys**: A root account is one that has unrestricted access to all AWS resources in your account. It is recommended that you delete access keys, access key IDs, and the secret access key for the root account so that they cannot be misused. Instead, create a user with the desired permissions and carry on tasks with this user.

- **Enforce MFA**: Add an additional layer of security by enforcing MFA for all privileged users having access to critical or sensitive resources and APIs having a high blast radius.

- **Use roles instead of users**: Roles are managed by AWS; they are preferred over IAM users, as credentials for roles are managed by AWS. These credentials are rotated multiple times in a day and not stored locally on your AWS resource such as an EC2 instance.

- **Use access advisor periodically**: You should periodically verify that all users having access to your AWS account are using their access privileges as assigned. If you find that users are not using their privilege for a defined period by running the access advisor report, then you should revoke that privilege and remove the unused credentials. The following figure shows the security status as per AWS recommended IAM best practices in the AWS Management Console:

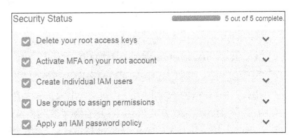

Figure 2: AWS IAM security best practices

VPC

VPC is your own virtual, secured, scalable network in the AWS cloud that contains your AWS resources. Let us look at the VPC security best practices:

- **Create custom VPC**: It is recommended to create your own VPC and not use the default VPC as it has default settings to allow unrestricted inbound and outbound traffic.

- **Monitor VPC activity**: Create VPC flow logs to monitor flow of all IP traffic in your VPC from network resources to identify and restrict any unwanted activity.

- **Use Network Address Translation (NAT)**: Keep all your resources that do not need access to the internet in a private subnet. Use a NAT device, such as a NAT instance or NAT gateway to allow internet access to resources in a private subnet.

- **Control access**: Use IAM to control access to the VPC and resources that are part of the VPC. You can create a fine grained access control using IAM for resources in your VPC.

- **Use NACL**: Configure NACLs to define which traffic is allowed and denied for your VPC through the subnet. Control inbound and outbound traffic for your VPC. Use NACL to block traffic from specific IPs or range of IPs by blacklisting them.

- **Implement IDS/IPS**: Use AWS solutions for **Intrusion Detection System (IDS)** and **Intrusion Prevention System (IPS)** or reach out to AWS partners at the AWS marketplace to secure your VPC through one of these systems.

- **Isolate VPCs**: Create separate VPCs as per your use cases to reduce the blast radius in the event of an incident. For example, create separate VPCs for your development, testing, and production environments.

- **Secure VPC**: Utilize the web application firewall, firewall virtual appliance, and firewall solutions from the AWS marketplace to secure your VPC. Configure site to site VPN for securely transferring data between your on-premise data center and the AWS VPC. Use the VPC peering feature to enable communication between two VPCs in the same region. Place ELB in a public subnet and all other EC2 instances in a private subnet unless they need to access the internet by these instances.

- **Tier security groups**: Use different security groups for various tiers of your architecture. For example, have a security group for your web servers and have another one for database servers. Use security groups for allowing access instead of hard coded IP ranges while configuring security groups.